Complete
EnglishSmart®

GRADE 8

Contents

Section 4   Writing

Dear Parent,

Thank you for choosing our *Complete EnglishSmart* as your child's learning companion.

We are confident that *Complete EnglishSmart* is the ultimate supplementary workbook your child needs to build upon his or her English language skills.

Complete EnglishSmart explores the fundamental aspects of language development – listening comprehension, grammar, reading, and writing – by introducing each concept with an easy-to-understand definition and clear examples. This is followed by a variety of interesting activities to provide plenty of practice for your child. There is also a note box at the end of each unit for your child to note down what he or she has learned.

To further ensure that your child retains the language concepts and enjoys the material, there is a review at the end of each section and also a Creative Corner section at the end of the book to help your child consolidate the language concepts in a fun and meaningful way. The accompanying online audio clips let your child practise and develop his or her listening skills.

We hope that your child will have fun learning and developing his or her English language skills with our *Complete EnglishSmart*.

Your Partner in Education,
Popular Book Company (Canada) Limited

Section 1

Listening Comprehension

UNIT

1

A Cross-Canada Culinary Tour

 This passage explores the different types of food that can be found in Canada. You will learn about the specialties of each region, how some food became the specialty of that region, and the diversity of Canada's foods, cultures, and people.

 **1.1** Read the questions in this unit before listening. Take notes as you listen. You may read the listening script on pages 188 and 189 if needed.

Keywords	Notes
distinct	
diversity	
exemplify	
haggis	
assortment	
regional	
specialty	
culinary	
partake	
fiddlehead	
casserole	
poutine	
bannock	
perogy	
dim sum	
cuisine	

A. Read the questions. Then check the correct answers.

1. If you were to travel coast to coast in Canada, what would you find?

   Ⓐ a wide and delicious assortment of regional specialties

   Ⓑ similar foods of one food type

   Ⓒ identical geography and politics across the nation

   Ⓓ one food that exemplifies all of Canada

2. What would a home-style meal in Newfoundland consist of?

   Ⓐ haggis and spaghetti

   Ⓑ baked codfish and blueberry pie

   Ⓒ bannock and berry pie

   Ⓓ baked bean casserole and poutine

3. Which province is known as Canada's "cattle country"?

   Ⓐ Alberta   Ⓑ New Brunswick

   Ⓒ Saskatchewan   Ⓓ Manitoba

4. Which cuisines is Vancouver famous for?

   Ⓐ Japanese and Polish cuisines

   Ⓑ Italian and Ukrainian cuisines

   Ⓒ French and Japanese cuisines

   Ⓓ Chinese and South Asian cuisines

B. Listen to the questions and answer options. Then write the correct letters in the boxes.

1.2

 ❶

❷

❸

❹

C. Fill in the blanks with the correct words from the passage.

1. Canada is divided into many regions based on _____ , politics, and ethnic communities.

2. The wide-ranging food specialties of Canada reflect the country's _____ .

3. Canada has a wide and delicious _____ of food specialties.

4. The baked bean casserole in _____ has a hint of sweet maple.

5. Granville Island Market is located in _____ .

6. _____ is French fries topped with brown gravy and cheese curds.

D. Answer the questions.

1. Why does Canada not have one food specialty?

    _____

    _____

    _____

2. Describe the food specialty of Manitoba.

    _____

    _____

    _____

3. Why do you think it would be easy to find diverse cuisine in any large Canadian city?

    _____

    _____

    _____

E. **Listen to the passage "A Cross-Canada Culinary Tour" again. Then write a summary in no more than 120 words.**

1.1

Include only the main points in the summary. Use your own words.

Summary

_____

_____

_____

_____

_____

_____

_____

_____

_____

_____

My Notes

_____

_____

_____

_____

UNIT 2

Surprising Stories about Sound

This passage explains general facts about sound and the human ear. You will learn about the workings and features of the human ear, the mechanics of sound, and the difference between humans' and animals' hearing.

2.1 Read the questions in this unit before listening. Take notes as you listen. You may read the listening script on pages 190 and 191 if needed.

Keywords	Notes

Keywords

sound

vibration

decode

pinna

auricle

ear canal

eardrum

ossicle

hammer

anvil

stirrup

magnify

cochlea

sensory cell

auditory nerve

hertz

frequency

A.   Read the questions. Then check the correct answers.

1.   What is another name for the pinna?

   Ⓐ ossicle   Ⓑ eardrum

   Ⓒ cochlea   Ⓓ auricle

2.   What do the ossicles consist of?

   Ⓐ the eardrum, anvil, and stirrup

   Ⓑ the hammer, anvil, and cochlea

   Ⓒ the hammer, anvil, and stirrup

   Ⓓ the ear canal, anvil, and stirrup

3.   What frequency can elephants hear?

   Ⓐ as low as two hertz

   Ⓑ as low as five hertz

   Ⓒ as high as 20 000 hertz

   Ⓓ as high as 200 000 hertz

4.   What is the purpose of the "Mosquito" tone?

   Ⓐ to win a Nobel Prize

   Ⓑ to prove that adults hear better than young people

   Ⓒ to attract young people and adult shoppers to convenience stores

   Ⓓ to disperse young people lingering in front of convenience stores while leaving adults unaffected

B.   Listen to the questions and answer options. Then write the correct letters in the boxes.

2.2   ❶ ⬚   ❷ ⬚   ❸ ⬚   ❹ ⬚

C.   Write "T" for the true statements and "F" for the false ones.

1.   The part of the ear that is visible is the pinna.   _____

2.   There are sensory cells inside the cochlea.   _____

3.   A tsunami is caused by an earthquake on the ocean floor.   _____

4.   Only elephants can detect tsunami vibrations.   _____

5.   As we age, we hear higher frequency sounds.   _____

6.   The "Mosquito" tone won a Nobel Prize.   _____

D.   Answer the questions.

1.   Explain how the human ear hears sound.

_____

_____

_____

_____

_____

2.   Can animals hear better than humans? Give an example from the passage.

_____

_____

_____

3.   In your opinion, is it right for convenience store owners to use the "Mosquito" tone to disperse young people? Why or why not?

_____

_____

_____

E. **Listen to the passage "Surprising Stories about Sound" again. Then write a summary in no more than 120 words.**

2.1

Include only the main points in the summary. Use your own words.

Summary

_____

_____

_____

_____

_____

_____

_____

_____

_____

My Notes

_____

_____

_____

_____

UNIT 3 The World of Tea

This passage explains general facts about tea, the second most-consumed drink in the world. You will learn about the four main types of tea, how they are made, where each type originated, where each type is popular, and the benefits of drinking tea.

3.1 Read the questions in this unit before listening. Take notes as you listen. You may read the listening script on pages 192 and 193 if needed.

Keywords	Notes
beverage	
satisfying	
oolong	
process	
oxidation	
fermentation	
wither	
delicate	
herbal	
Camellia sinensis	
cardamom	
tapioca	
bergamot	
matcha	
novelty	
versatile	

A. Read the questions. Then check the correct answers.

1. What are the main types of tea?

    Ⓐ black, white, brown, and green

    Ⓑ green, oolong, chai, and herbal

    Ⓒ herbal, matcha, chai, and oolong

    Ⓓ black, white, green, and oolong

2. Which tea is often referred to as the "Champagne of Teas"?

    Ⓐ black tea   Ⓑ white tea

    Ⓒ green tea   Ⓓ oolong tea

3. Which tea is high in vitamins A, B, C, E, and K?

    Ⓐ Darjeeling   Ⓑ matcha

    Ⓒ chai   Ⓓ bubble tea

4. Which description best defines Earl Grey tea?

    Ⓐ It is withered and dried, has a pale green colour, and has a delicate taste.

    Ⓑ It is mixed with cold milk and dollops of tapioca balls.

    Ⓒ It is made from bright green tea leaf powder that is not oxidized.

    Ⓓ It is a blend of black teas mixed with bergamot oil.

B. Listen to the questions and answer options. Then write the correct letters in the boxes.

3.2

 1

 2

 3

 4

C.   Write to match the teas with their descriptions.

> **Earl Grey   bubble tea   herbal tea   oolong**
> **chai   mint tea**

1.   Peppermint tea is a popular tea of this type.   _____

2.   This tea contains tapioca balls and it is popular in
     Hong Kong, Taiwan, and Singapore.   _____

3.   This tea is popular in North Africa and in the
     Middle East.   _____

4.   This is the second most popular black tea in the world.   _____

5.   Do not drink this tea with milk, sugar, or lemon.   _____

6.   This tea is made with cardamom, ginger, cinnamon,
     fennel, and cloves.   _____

D.   Answer the questions.

1.   How did tea originate and how has it become a worldwide demand?

     _____

     _____

2.   Explain the differences among the four main types of tea.

     _____

     _____

     _____

     _____

3.   What is flowering tea?

     _____

     _____

     _____

E. **Listen to the passage "The World of Tea" again. Then write a summary in no more than 120 words.**

3.1

Include only the main points in the summary. Use your own words.

Summary

_____

_____

_____

_____

_____

_____

_____

_____

_____

My Notes

_____

_____

_____

_____

UNIT 4

Another "Ice Age" on the Way?

This passage explains general facts about ice ages and global warming. You will learn about the causes and effects of ice ages and global warming, as well as some of the theories behind the occurrence of ice ages. You will also learn about the water currents that affect and are affected by ice ages and global warming.

4.1 Read the questions in this unit before listening. Take notes as you listen. You may read the listening script on pages 194 and 195 if needed.

Keywords	Notes
inexorable	
greenhouse effect	
significant	
glacier	
theorize	
encase	
permafrost	
plausible	
demise	
reservoir	
current	
conveyor belt	
latitude	
unprecedented	
disrupt	

A. **Read the questions. Then check the correct answers.**

1. When did "The Little Ice Age" occur?

   (A) in 1300
   (B) in 1870
   (C) around 1300 to 1870
   (D) 8200 years ago

2. By how much did the temperature drop during "The Little Ice Age"?

   (A) about 1°C
   (B) about 2°C
   (C) 3°C
   (D) more than 4°C

3. What is North America's glacial reservoir called?

   (A) the Gulf Stream
   (B) Lake Agassiz
   (C) Lake Winnipeg
   (D) the North Atlantic Basin

4. Why do certain islands along the coast of Scotland have palm trees and why does Iceland have a relatively mild climate?

   (A) It is because of global warming.
   (B) These are the consequences of an ice age.
   (C) It is due to the warming effect of the Gulf Stream.
   (D) It is because of carbon dioxide emissions.

B. **Listen to the questions and answer options. Then write the correct letters in the boxes.**

4.2

 1

 2

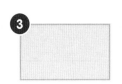 3

 4

C. Fill in the blanks with words from the passage.

1. Some scientists and environmentalists say that _____ may bring another ice age.

2. During "The Little Ice Age", _____ advanced onto the farmland in Norway.

3. "The Little Ice Age" caused _____ in parts of Europe.

4. Frozen bodies of woolly mammoths can be found in the permafrost of

    _____ .

5. _____ was drained when the Laurentide Ice Sheet in northeastern North America collapsed.

6. _____ is a remnant of North America's glacial reservoir.

7. The glaciers of Greenland are _____ at an unprecedented rate.

8. Despite its high latitude, Iceland's climate is

    relatively _____ .

Iceland

D. Answer the questions.

1. What is one theory of the cause of "The Little Ice Age"?

    _____

    _____

2. Describe what the Gulf Stream is.

    _____

    _____

    _____

E. **Listen to the passage "Another 'Ice Age' on the Way?" again. Then write a summary in no more than 120 words.**

4.1

Include only the main points in the summary. Use your own words.

Summary

_____

_____

_____

_____

_____

_____

_____

_____

_____

_____

My Notes

_____

_____

_____

_____

UNIT

5 Special Olympians

 This passage explains general facts about the Special Olympics. You will learn about the history of the events and the Olympians who have participated and won. The benefits of participating in and the importance of hosting this event are also explored.

5.1 Read the questions in this unit before listening. Take notes as you listen. You may read the listening script on pages 196 and 197 if needed.

Keywords	Notes
anticipated	
athlete	
achievement	
revolutionize	
conventional	
participate	
international	
intellectual	
disability	
physically	
elite	
alternate	
agency	
professional	
cognitive	
vocational	
spiritually	

A. Read the questions. Then check the correct answers.

1. Who was the "Flying Dutchwoman"?

   (A) Fanny Blankers-Koen

   (B) Tessa Virtue

   (C) Christine Sinclair

   (D) Clara Hughes

2. When was the Special Olympics founded?

   (A) in 1936   (B) in 1948

   (C) in 1968   (D) in 1930

3. When are the Special Olympic Games held?

   (A) before the Olympics

   (B) during the Olympics

   (C) after the Olympics

   (D) every summer and winter

4. What is the Fosbury Flop?

   (A) It is a way to do the high jump by jumping over the bar backward.

   (B) It is the nickname of Richard Fosbury.

   (C) It is an organization for Olympians who participate in the high jump.

   (D) It is the name of a high jump instructor.

B. Listen to the questions and answer options. Then write the correct letters in the boxes.

5.2

1

2

3

4

C.   Write "T" for the true statements and "F" for the false ones.

1.   Jesse Owens won four gold medals at the 1936 Berlin Olympic Games.   _____

2.   Fanny Blankers-Koen won four gold medals in 1948.   _____

3.   Patrick Chan and Clara Hughes are Canadian Olympians.   _____

4.   The Special Olympics is a national organization in the United States.   _____

5.   The first event of the Special Olympics was held the year after the organization was founded.   _____

6.   The Special Olympics World Summer and Winter Games alternate every two years.   _____

7.   Millions of athletes in over 170 countries train with the Special Olympics.   _____

8.   Participants of all ages can join the Special Olympics.   _____

D.   Answer the questions.

1.   What are the Special Olympics?

    _____

    _____

    _____

2.   Who can participate in the Special Olympics?

    _____

    _____

    _____

3.   What are the benefits of participating in the Special Olympics?

    _____

    _____

    _____

E. **Listen to the passage "Special Olympians" again. Then write a summary in no more than 120 words.**

5.1

Include only the main points in the summary. Use your own words.

Summary

_____

_____

_____

_____

_____

_____

_____

_____

_____

My Notes

_____

_____

_____

_____

The Rafflesia – a True Floral Wonder

This passage describes the Rafflesia. You will learn about its "discovery", where it can be found, and its unique characteristics. You will also learn about its significance to Southeast Asian countries.

Read the questions in this review before listening. Take notes as you listen. You may read the listening script on pages 198 and 199 if needed.

Notes

A. Circle the answers.

1. The Rafflesia is the _____ flower in the world.

   smallest

   largest

   deadliest

   most fragrant

2. In which year was the Rafflesia first documented in English?

   1818

   1828

   1830

   1880

3. The Rafflesia can only be found in _____ countries.

   West Asian

   Central Asian

   Southeast Asian

   South Asian

4. How many species of Rafflesia are there?

   10

   12

   15

   more than 15

5. The Rafflesia is a _____ .

   poisonous plant

   fungus

   parasitic plant

   parasitic root

6. To which plant does the Rafflesia adhere itself?

   the Tetrastigma vine

   the Tetrastigma fungus

   the Tetrastigma flower

   the Tetrastigma root

7. How many petals does the Rafflesia have?

   four

   five

   six

   seven

8. How long does it take for the Rafflesia to grow to its full size?

   about three months

   about six months

   about nine months

   about one year

B. Listen to the questions and answer options. Then write the correct letters in the boxes.

 1  **2**  **3**  **4**

R1.2

C. Write "T" for the true statements and "F" for the false ones.

1. Sir Thomas Stamford Raffles founded the city of Singapore. _____

2. A Rafflesia in bloom gives off an odour akin to rotting meat or even human decomposition. _____

3. The Rafflesia does not depend on another plant to thrive and grow. _____

4. The Rafflesia has no stem, no leaves, and no roots. _____

5. The Rafflesia is the official state flower of Singapore in Malaysian Borneo. _____

6. The Rafflesia is the official provincial flower of Surat Thani, Indonesia. _____

D. Write the information to complete the sentences.

1. Dr. Joseph Arnold is the British naturalist who _____

   _____.

2. The most striking thing about the Rafflesia _____

   _____.

3. The Tetrastigma vine has a special fungus-like tissue _____

   _____.

4. So famous and rare is the Rafflesia _____

   _____.

E. **Read the following lecture notes on the Rafflesia. Rewrite them so they are true. Then research and write one more fact about the Rafflesia.**

Dec. 14, 2019

The Rafflesia

1. The flower can only be found in Southeast Asian countries including India, Malaysia, Thailand, and the Philippines.

2. The smell of the Rafflesia attracts the flower's pollinators, such as butterflies and bees.

3. Because of its size and strength, the Rafflesia's life is long-lived.

4. Nature enthusiasts, as well as tourists, visit the mountains of Southeast Asia to see the Rafflesia in bloom.

1. _____

_____

2. _____

_____

3. _____

_____

4. _____

_____

My Research

_____

_____

F.　Fill in the blanks of this postcard with the correct information.

Dear Janice,

Exploring this r_____ in l_____ has been exhilarating. Our guide showed us the infamous R_____ – the l_____ flower in the world! Everything I have ever heard about its p_____ s_____ is true! I can see why its name means "m_____ flower" or "c_____ flower" in local S_____ A_____ languages. I will write again soon.

Sincerely,

Elsa

Your stamp here

To:

Janice Steward

219 Seaside Road

NS Canada

G.　Check the true statements.

Characteristics of the Rafflesia

1.　☐　The Rafflesia's petals are usually white with red spots.

　　☐　The Rafflesia's petals are usually red with white spots.

2.　☐　The Rafflesia can grow up to 106 m in diameter.

　　☐　The Rafflesia can grow up to 106 cm in diameter.

3.　☐　The Rafflesia can weigh up to 10 kilograms.

　　☐　The Rafflesia can weigh up to 20 kilograms.

H. Answer the questions.

1. Why does the Rafflesia depend on another plant to thrive and grow?

   _____

   _____

2. How does the Tetrastigma vine enable the Rafflesia to grow?

   _____

   _____

3. Why are all known species of the Rafflesia threatened or endangered?

   _____

I. Listen to the passage "The Rafflesia – a True Floral Wonder" again. Then write a summary in no more than 120 words.

R1.1

Listen carefully to make sure you catch all of the important points of the passage to include them in your summary. Use your own words.

Summary

_____

_____

_____

_____

_____

_____

_____

_____

_____

Section 2

Grammar

UNIT

1

Prepositional and Phrasal Verbs

A **prepositional verb** is a verb that is followed by a preposition. It needs an object, which always comes immediately after the preposition.

Examples

- She <u>talks to</u> him every day.
- Have you <u>looked at</u> your report card yet?

A. Write the prepositions that go with the following verbs.

1. belong _____
2. listen _____
3. hint _____
4. worry _____
5. sympathize _____
6. lead _____
7. stare _____
8. consist _____
9. refer _____
10. scoff _____
11. depend _____

B. Underline the prepositional verbs in the sentences.

1. When I was younger, I believed in the tooth fairy.

2. She vowed to never speak to him again.

3. I don't think I can rely on him anymore.

4. The rowdy boys always joke about silly things.

5. Bobby apologized for the mess he had made.

6. When the clown pretended to trip, everyone laughed at him.

7. Lily and I had an argument because I disagreed with her.

8. She is a good nurse because she cares about her patients.

9. Did you hear about the requirements for entering the contest?

10. Last night I dreamed about going to the beach.

A **phrasal verb** contains a verb and an adverb or a preposition or both. It can extend the meaning of the verb or create a whole new meaning.

Unlike prepositional verbs, not all phrasal verbs need an object. For some phrasal verbs that take an object, the object can come before or after the adverb. If the object is a pronoun, the adverb always comes after it.

Examples

- Without an object:
  (set out = start a journey)
  Hank <u>set out</u> in the morning.

- With an object:
  (leave out = omit)
  You can <u>leave out</u> this part.
  You can <u>leave</u> this part <u>out</u>.
  You can <u>leave</u> it <u>out</u>.

C. Circle the correct phrasal verbs to complete the sentences.

1. The firefighters _____ the fire quickly.

   put on   put out   put up

2. Matt could not _____ the answer.

   figure out   figure up   figure for

3. I have to _____ this word. I have no idea what it means.

   look at   look for   look up

4. Marie is so fast that it is difficult to _____ her.

   keep up with   keep up for   keep in with

5. Don't _____ the answer now. Give me some time to solve it.

   give out   give in   give away

6. They had to _____ the meeting because of the power outage.

   call up   call in   call off

7. Tamar _____ a great idea for the show.

   came up with   came in with   came up by

8. Someone _____ our neighbours' house when they went out for dinner last night.

   broke up   broke into   broke out

D. **Identify the meanings of the phrasal verbs. Write the letters in the parentheses.**

1. **turn down** Ⓐ reduce Ⓑ reject; not accept

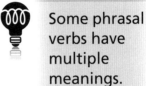

Some phrasal verbs have multiple meanings.

  a. Miranda turned down ( ) the offer and left immediately.

  b. Could you please turn down ( ) the volume?

2. **bring up** Ⓐ raise; care for Ⓑ mention in conversation

  a. The children were brought up ( ) on a farm.

  b. Lester brought up ( ) his innovative idea in the conference.

3. **pass out** Ⓐ distribute Ⓑ faint

  a. Please help me pass out ( ) these flyers.

  b. The girl looked pale and she suddenly passed out ( ).

4. **work out** Ⓐ exercise Ⓑ succeed

  a. Did your plan work out ( )?

  b. My sister works out ( ) in the gym every day.

E. **Write a sentence of your own for each meaning of the phrasal verb.**

take off

Ⓐ start to fly: _____

_____

Ⓑ remove: _____

_____

Ⓒ leave hastily:_____

_____

F. **Fill in the blanks to complete the prepositional verbs and phrasal verbs. Then identify them by writing their sentence numbers in the correct boxes.**

1. Jack was not paying attention and he bumped _____ a pole.

2. Let's hope _____ the best.

3. What does "UNESCO" stand _____ ?

4. Samantha is suffering _____ a fever.

5. Never ever look down _____ others.

6. The gardener cares _____ all his flowers.

7. They insisted _____ inviting Clare to the meeting.

8. She is trying to make _____ all the lost time.

9. My mother drops me _____ at school every morning.

10. Luke is deciding _____ which car to buy.

11. The ice cream machine suddenly broke _____ .

12. His rudeness in the incident put everyone _____ .

13. I may or may not go, depending _____ the weather.

14. It is too noisy to make _____ what the guest speaker is saying.

15. The suspect insisted that he was set _____ by his friend.

Prepositional Verb

Phrasal Verb

My Notes

_____

_____

_____

_____

UNIT
2 Finite and Non-finite Verbs

A **finite verb** is a verb that shows the tense and agrees with the subject in number. It is the main verb in a sentence and usually follows the subject.

Examples

• She <u>enjoys</u> playing in the snow.
  ↑ present tense; singular verb form

• We <u>were</u> happy to meet again.
  ↑ past tense; plural verb form

A. Check if the underlined verbs are finite verbs. Put a cross if they are not.

1. We <u>looked</u> at our family photos together last night. _____

2. She waited eagerly for the parcel <u>to arrive</u>. _____

3. Andrew <u>wants</u> to play with his friends in the park. _____

4. Janice left the party early so that she <u>could</u> catch the last bus. _____

5. <u>Wearing</u> the same cap to the gathering was Sammy's suggestion. _____

B. Write above the underlined finite verbs to correct them. Then circle the changes made.

Changes in

1. Jessica <u>walk</u> to school with her neighbour every day.

   tense / agreement

2. Stephen <u>stop</u> by the coffee shop to get some drinks on his way home yesterday.

   tense / agreement

3. Last night, our family <u>stay</u> up late to plan for our vacation.

   tense / agreement

4. Tracy and I <u>am</u> best friends and we care about each other's feelings.

   tense / agreement

5. The children <u>has</u> to get their parents' permission before they can participate in the game.

   tense / agreement

A **non-finite verb** is a verb that does not have to agree with the subject and is not the main verb in a sentence. It can be a participle, a gerund, or an infinitive.

A **participle** is the present participle form (ends in "ing") or the past participle form (usually ends in "ed") of a verb that functions as an adjective.

- Macy solved the <u>challenging</u> riddle.
  present participle

- The <u>exhausted</u> players
  past participle
  went home.

C. Circle the correct participles for the sentences.

1. We have not played with the **won / winning** team this season.

2. The **trapped / trapping** kitten trembled with fear and waited desperately for help.

3. Frightened by the **barked / barking** dog, the stranger ran away.

4. Surrounded by her **excited / exciting** fans, the pop star promised to sing a song from her latest album.

5. The **inspired / inspiring** speech encouraged everyone to volunteer.

6. **Sped / Speeding** motorists will be stopped and fined.

7. Satisfied with Ben's results, Ms. Watts agreed to let him join her **promised / promising** team.

8. A **refreshed / refreshing** breeze blew over the beach.

9. The **finished / finishing** paintings will be displayed in the museum downtown.

10. The **giggled / giggling** toddlers are having great fun in the park.

11. The police found the **stolen / stealing** car in a **deserted / deserting** farmhouse.

12. The **entertained / entertaining** show lasted almost two hours.

A **gerund** is the "ing" form of a verb that functions as a noun. It can act as the subject or the object in a sentence.

Example

<u>Driving</u> is fun but it requires
subject

<u>practising</u>.
object

D. **Fill in the blanks with the correct gerunds. Then write "S" if they act as subjects and "O" if they act as objects in the boxes.**

> hike   laugh   write
> recycle   cook

1. _____ ☐ is a simple way to help save natural resources.

2. _____ ☐ relieves stress and lifts your mood.

3. Have you finished _____ ☐ your story.

4. Let's go _____ ☐ this Saturday morning.

5. Mom enjoys _____ ☐ for us after a day's work.

E. **Rewrite the sentences by replacing the underlined words with gerunds. Make any other necessary changes.**

1. <u>A jump</u> over the ditch can be dangerous.

   _____

   _____

2. He sustained a severe injury as a result of <u>the fall</u>.

   _____

   _____

3. <u>A loss</u> in the eighth inning upset the game plan.

   _____

4. <u>An increase</u> in the use of fuel leads to more pollution.

   _____

An **infinitive** is a verb that functions as a noun, an adjective, or an adverb in a sentence. It is formed with "to" followed by the base form of a verb.

- <u>To indulge</u> would be a luxury.
  noun

- He always brings along a book <u>to read</u>.
  adjective

- <u>To win</u>, we need to have confidence.
  adverb

F. **Complete the sentences with appropriate infinitives. Then write the sentence numbers in the correct boxes to show what the infinitives function as.**

1. _____ would be a challenge for all of us.

2. What I want to do most is _____ .

3. Mr. Ward has some tasks _____ before he retires.

4. _____ , we have to seek help from the committee members.

5. All the spectators stayed until the soccer game was over

   _____ .

6. Morning is the best time

   _____ .

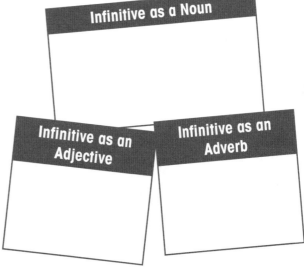

Infinitive as a Noun

Infinitive as an Adjective

Infinitive as an Adverb

My Notes

_____

_____

_____

_____

UNIT

3 **Non-progressive Verbs**

Non-progressive verbs are non-action verbs that:

- describe senses, emotional and mental states, possession, and existence.
- cannot be used in the continuous tense.

Examples

- She is seeming nice. ✗
  She <u>seems</u> nice. ✔

- It is smelling delicious. ✗
  It <u>smells</u> delicious. ✔

A. **Underline the verbs that should not be in the continuous tense. Rewrite above them so that they are correct.**

1. I am seeing the teacher walk toward his office.

2. The apple pies in the oven are smelling wonderful.

 Some non-progressive verbs that indicate senses:

feel, see, smell, taste, hear

3. Are you hearing that? It is coming from outside.

4. Even with his thick coat on, Pete still is not feeling warm.

5. Mona and Betsy are feeling guilty for forgetting their friend's birthday.

6. When I was tidying my room, I was hearing my neighbour practise the trumpet.

7. The soup is not tasting good so I am going to add some herbs to make it tastier.

8. Joyce was seeing a man outside the theatre but she did not notice that he was a movie star.

9. We were feeling hungry after working out for two hours.

10. Uncle Steve was tasting the curry when he finished cooking to make sure it was not too spicy for us.

11. Miranda likes putting plants in her room. It is smelling like a garden.

B. Circle the correct non-progressive verbs that indicate emotional states to complete the sentences.

1. Joshua **likes / dislikes** swimming so he practises swimming every day.

2. My helpful family and friends are the ones I **need / envy** .

3. After looking at all the options, they **preferred / wished** taking the bus to their destination.

4. I **appreciate / want** your thoughtfulness in preparing refreshments for the event.

5. Gina **needs / hates** wasting food so she always finishes everything on her plate.

6. The children **disliked / wished** the heavy rain would stop soon so they could go outside and play.

7. Keith's mom **loves / fears** basketball and she never misses watching any game when it is broadcast on TV.

8. Little Jane **envied / delighted** everyone by playing a happy tune on the piano.

C. Complete the sentences with the given non-progressive verbs that indicate emotional states.

1. **miss**

   My best friend has moved to Edmonton _____ .

2. **fear**

   Clare did not give up although _____ .

3. **wonder**

   The task seems impossible _____ .

D.   Fill in the blanks with the correct forms of the non-progressive verbs that indicate mental states.

1.   Amy's parents _____ (believe) she can achieve her dream if she tries hard enough.

>
> Non-progressive verbs that indicate mental states are verbs that show how the subject of a sentence thinks.

2.   Eli always _____ (forget) to bring his keys with him and locks himself out.

3.   Scientists _____ (imagine) that we will be able to move to different planets in the future.

4.   I _____ (doubt) he will be here on time because he is always late.

5.   When it started raining, Ken _____ (realize) that he had left his umbrella in the café.

6.   We all _____ (suppose) Bill will join the event because he is one of the organizers.

7.   Landon _____ (think) that his sister is upset with him because she is ignoring him.

8.   Both my brother and I have grown up so much that our aunt hardly _____ (recognize) us at the family party last night.

9.   Most of the students who attended the ceremony _____ (agree) with the guest speaker's opinion on moral education.

10.   Hailey always _____ (remember) to bring along her lunch to school.

11.   Wesley loves reading fantasy stories and he _____ (believe) fantasy creatures like elves and dragons do exist.

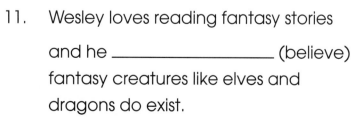

Non-progressive verbs that indicate possession are verbs that show whom or what the subject has, or who or what possesses the subject.

Non-progressive verbs that indicate existence are verbs that show how the subject is or is perceived to be.

E. Circle the specified non-progressive verbs in the sentences. Then write sentences of your own using the circled verbs.

Non-progressive Verbs Indicating Possession

1. Micah has a pet dog and he is walking it in the park now.

   _____

2. Do you see the painting over there? It belongs to Mr. Sze.

   _____

Non-progressive Verbs Indicating Existence

3. The lunch we are going to order includes a sandwich and a drink.

   _____

4. The storybook that Janice picked contains more than 300 pages.

   _____

My Notes

_____

_____

_____

_____

UNIT

4 **Modal Verbs**

A **modal verb** is an auxiliary verb that:

- cannot be the main verb in a sentence.
- is used to express permission, ability, possibility, obligation, and more.
- is followed by a bare infinitive (a verb without "to").

Examples

- Permission: You <u>may</u> leave now.
- Ability: I <u>can</u> dance.
- Possibility: He <u>might</u> visit again.
- Obligation: You <u>must</u> wait here.

A. **Circle the modal verbs and underline the bare infinitives in the sentences. Then write what the modal verbs express on the lines.**

What Modal Verbs Express

permission	ability	possibility	obligation
suggestion	advice	certainty	request

1. Newborn polar bear cubs cannot see. _____

2. You should try to open your mind if you want to be more creative. _____

3. If you have time tonight, could you give me a hand with the cooking? _____

4. We could have breakfast in the hotel before visiting the museum. _____

5. Once I have got my chores done, I can play basketball with my friends. _____

6. Pedestrians should always look both ways before crossing the road. _____

7. Sasha may not be able to join us for dinner because she has to babysit her neighbour's daughter. _____

8. Natalie and Benjamin will take part in the charity run this Saturday. _____

"Can", **"could"**, and **"may"** can be used to give or ask for **permission**. "Could" and "may" are more formal and polite than "can".

Questions with modal verbs are formed by inversion.

Examples

- You <u>can</u> use the pen over there.
- You and your sister <u>could</u> share the room.
- We <u>may</u> leave earlier.
- <u>May</u> I join your team?

B. For each situation, write a question asking for permission and an answer giving permission.

1. You and your classmates want to ask the guest speaker, Mr. Torres, some more questions.

    You: _____

    _____

    Mr. Torres: _____

    _____

2. You forgot to bring your pencil case and would like to borrow a pencil from your classmate, Elena.

    You: _____

    Elena: _____

3. It is raining heavily and you would like to ask if your friend's mom, Mrs. Ross, could give you a ride home.

    You: _____

    Mrs. Ross: _____

4. You want very much to watch a baseball game on TV but your mom is watching her favourite drama series.

    You: _____

    Your mom: _____

Section **2**

Grammar

Examples

"**May**", "**might**", "**could**", and "**can**" can be used to show **possibility**.

For something possible but not certain:

may, might, could

For something generally possible:

can

- Mom <u>may</u> buy some desserts for us.
- Benjamin <u>might</u> get himself into trouble.
- This <u>could</u> be the only solution to the problem.
- It <u>can</u> be very windy in the open ocean.

C.   **Write answers to the questions using modal verbs of possibility.**

1. Jen is on a crowded bus. What do you think makes her happy?

   _____

   _____

2. Adrian has lost his key. Where do you think it is?

   _____

3. Mr. Barnes has missed the last train home. What do you think he will do?

   _____

4. The hikers have reached a mountain peak. What do you think the weather is like there?

   _____

5. Isabel likes outdoor activities. What do you think she will do this Saturday?

   _____

6. It has been snowing for the whole week. When do you think the snow will stop?

   _____

7. The children are on a farm. What do you think they will do there?

   _____

D. **The word in parentheses at the end of each sentence shows what the modal verb should express. Check the circle if the modal verb is correct. If not, rewrite the sentence with the correct modal verb.**

1. If you play in the sun, you may wear a cap. (advice)

   _____

2. Since there is no school tomorrow, we should go to the movies. (suggestion) ○

   _____

3. Will I adopt a dog from the animal shelter? (formal request) ○

   _____

4. The clouds are dark. It can rain soon. (general possibility) ○

   _____

5. You must leave your bag in my office. (formal permission) ○

   _____

6. Everyone should help keep the classroom tidy. (obligation) ○

   _____

7. Mrs. Patterson might give a speech at the farewell party. (possibility) ○

   _____

8. Jessica must speak English, French, Spanish, and Japanese. (ability) ○

   _____

My Notes

_____

_____

_____

_____

UNIT 5 Order and Position of Adjectives

The usual order of adjectives is:

Function – Adjective

- Opinion – lovely, precious
- Size – tiny, huge
- Age – old, young
- Shape – round, rectangular
- Colour – red, blonde
- Origin – Canadian, European
- Material – plastic, silver
- Purpose – shopping, gardening

Examples

- Mia cherished the <u>pretty</u>, _{opinion} <u>antique</u> <u>gold</u> necklace from age material her grandma.

- He reuses the <u>large</u>, <u>green</u> size colour <u>shopping</u> bag. purpose

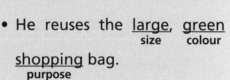

When there are multiple adjectives before a noun in a sentence, they are placed in a specific order based on their functions.

A. Underline the adjectives in the sentences and write their functions above them.

1. My mother bought a pair of new, white running shoes for me.

2. I broke my favourite, blue ceramic mug today.

3. The popular, young British singer is waving to her fans.

4. Joshua has a handsome, brown leather wallet.

5. Both Mr. and Mrs. Diaz like the big, round dining table.

6. There is a sparkling, heart-shaped diamond necklace in the display window.

7. Mimi's grandmother is a charming, petite French lady.

8. The small, old wooden house belongs to Farmer Cole.

B. Write the adjectives in the correct order. Then write the letters on the lines to put them in the correct sentences.

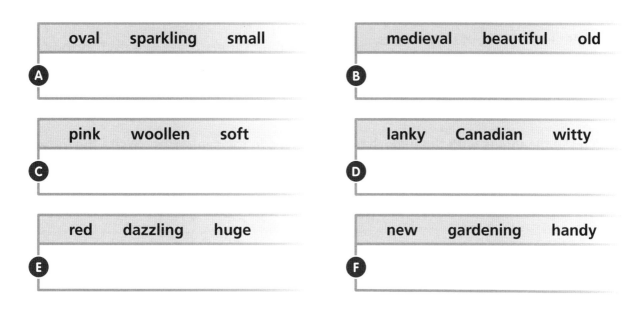

	oval sparkling small		medieval beautiful old
A		**B**	

	pink woollen soft		lanky Canadian witty
C		**D**	

	red dazzling huge		new gardening handy
E		**F**	

1. According to Jenny, the new teacher is a ⎯ gentleman.

2. The shop assistant showed Carmen a ⎯ gemstone.

3. After an hour's walk, we finally reached the ⎯ castle.

4. Mr. Buffet put the ⎯ tools in the box.

5. The setting sun is a ⎯ fireball.

6. She likes wearing that ⎯ coat in the cool weather.

C. Use three adjectives to describe each underlined noun to enrich the sentence.

1. They found a <u>hut</u> deep in the forest.

   _____

2. The <u>banner</u> caught our attention.

   _____

3. The <u>goose</u> came toward us.

   _____

Many adjectives can be put in front of the nouns they describe or after them without a change in meaning. For some adjectives, however, the change in position changes their meanings.

Examples

• The <u>present</u> situation worried him.
⌐—means: current

• The members <u>present</u> voted for him.
⌐—means: the members that were there

D. **Match the meanings with the underlined adjectives in the sentences. Write the letters in the parentheses.**

1. **responsible**: Ⓐ entrusted with as a duty   Ⓑ conscientious; having good judgment

    a. He is a <u>responsible</u> ( ) person.

    b. The officer <u>responsible</u> ( ) for the case was away.

2. **due**: Ⓐ expected; scheduled for   Ⓑ proper; appropriate

    a. This is the first payment <u>due</u> ( ).

    b. You should be driving with <u>due</u> ( ) care.

3. **involved**: Ⓐ complex   Ⓑ embroiled

    a. It was an <u>involved</u> ( ) discussion.

    b. The principal wants to see the students <u>involved</u> ( ) in the fight.

4. **concerned**: Ⓐ worried; anxious   Ⓑ affected; related; involved

    a. The people <u>concerned</u> ( ) did not say anything.

    b. The <u>concerned</u> ( ) mother rushed her son to the hospital.

5. **absent**: Ⓐ away; not present   Ⓑ not attentive; preoccupied

    a. Katherine answered my question with an <u>absent</u> ( ) nod.

    b. The employees <u>absent</u> ( ) today will not receive a bonus.

Putting adjectives after nouns:

- Some adjectives ending in "-able" or "-ible" can be used after nouns.
- Adjectives are put after words such as "someone", "everything", and "anywhere".
- Adjectives are placed after measurement nouns.
- Adjectives can be placed after the verb and its object in a sentence.

Examples

- This is the only dress <u>available</u>.
- I want to eat something <u>delicious</u>.
- The ribbon is one metre <u>long</u>.
- What made Adriana's cat <u>upset</u>?

E. Write two sentences with each adjective.

1. possible

   (before a noun) _____

   (after a noun) _____

2. happy

   (before a noun) _____

   (after "someone") _____

3. older

   (before a noun) _____

   (after a measurement noun) _____

4. messy

   (before a noun) _____

   (after a verb and its object) _____

My Notes

_____

_____

_____

_____

Section **2**

Grammar

UNIT

6 Correlative Conjunctions

Examples

Correlative conjunctions are pairs of words that connect two equivalent elements in a sentence, such as words, phrases, or clauses. Correlative conjunctions must always be used together. Some correlative conjunctions are:

either...or ← one of the options

neither...nor ← none of the options

not only...but also ← both of the options

whether...or ← regardless of the options

- <u>Either</u> Josh <u>or</u> Ben can take this seat.

- <u>Neither</u> your plan <u>nor</u> her plan is acceptable.

- <u>Not only</u> does she play the piano <u>but</u> she <u>also</u> plays the flute.

- She was going <u>whether</u> they liked it <u>or</u> not.

A.   Complete the sentences with the correct correlative conjunctions.

1.   _____ we go on the trip _____ not depends on my father.

2.   _____ Nikki _____ Hugh could explain clearly what happened.

3.   The teacher will most likely choose _____ Sarah _____ Sam to be the team leader.

4.   _____ was the cinematography great _____ the acting was _____ phenomenal.

5.   Regardless of _____ Lindy liked them _____ hated them, she had to finish her vegetables at dinner.

6.   The panel would consider _____ the scores _____ their overall performance in the interview.

7.   _____ Tien _____ Tyler knew what to do next.

8.   You can _____ have the chocolate cake _____ the strawberry cake but you cannot have both.

Other correlative conjunctions include:

- **both...and** ← includes both options

- **no sooner...than** ← expresses the idea that the second event appears right after the first

- **as...as** ← compares options

- **as many...as** ← compares the quantity of options

- **rather...than** ← expresses preference of one option over the other

- The movie was <u>both</u> funny <u>and</u> sad.

- <u>No sooner</u> had we arrived at the theatre <u>than</u> the movie began.

- Skating is not <u>as</u> fun <u>as</u> skiing.

- There are <u>as many</u> boys <u>as</u> there are girls here.

- I would <u>rather</u> have cake <u>than</u> ice cream.

B. Write the letters to match each sentence with the correct correlative conjunctions.

	Correlative Conjunctions
	A. both...and
	B. no sooner...than
	C. as...as
	D. as many...as
	E. rather...than

1. ◯ Nate would ____ play soccer ____ play hockey.

2. ◯ Mr. Knight is ____ a teacher ____ a coach.

3. ◯ No one in the class can run ____ fast ____ Dave.

4. ◯ The blue dress is not ____ pretty ____ the red dress.

5. ◯ He has ____ blue ties ____ he does grey ties.

6. ◯ She would not let me get ____ the shirt ____ the shoes.

7. ◯ ____ had Keith ended the phone call ____ the door bell rang.

8. ◯ Marco would ____ have a chocolate birthday cake ____ a vanilla one.

9. ◯ ____ had my dad stopped the car ____ our dog ran to welcome him home.

Amsterdam

10. ◯ Amsterdam is known as the bicycle capital of the world because there are ____ bicycles ____ there are people!

Section 2

Grammar

When using "either...or" and "neither...nor", there must be **pronoun-antecedent agreement**. An antecedent is the word, phrase, or clause to which a pronoun refers. With a compound subject joined by "or/nor" in a correlative conjunction, the pronoun must agree with the antecedent closer to the pronoun.

Examples

- Either Stephy or <u>I</u> will ask <u>my</u>

  antecedent ⟶   pronoun ⟶

  parents for permission.

- Neither Ava nor <u>her sisters</u> know

  antecedent ⟶

  why <u>their</u> parents said no.

  ↑
  pronoun

C.   Circle the correct pronouns to complete the sentences.

1. Neither my father nor his siblings remember where   **their / his**   old family photos are.

2. Either Malcolm or the other players will help   **their / his**   coach carry the equipment back to the storage room.

3. Neither Ben nor Betsy knew why   **his / her**   parents invited the neighbours to dinner.

4. Either Wendy or Omar will bring   **his / her**   board game to my place.

5. Neither Sarah nor Samuel brought   **his / her**   notebook to class.

6. Either Sheila or her classmates will buy   **their / her**   teacher a gift.

7. Neither we nor the girls wanted to clean   **our / their**   classroom after the party.

8. It was either Will or Kate who broke **his / her**   classroom's window.

9. It was neither Rachel nor Harry who stole **his / her**   mother's favourite necklace.

10. Neither Megan nor her siblings had **her / their**   suitcases packed for the trip.

When using "either...or" and "neither...nor", there must also be **subject-verb agreement**. This means that the verb that follows the correlative conjunction must agree in number with the subject closer to the verb. So, if the closer subject is singular, the singular form of the verb should be used. If it is plural, the plural form should be used.

Examples

- Either the guests or the host is going to give the opening speech.

- Neither Ken nor his friends were aware of the situation.

D. Check if the sentences have subject-verb agreement. If not, put a cross and rewrite the sentences so that they are correct.

1. Neither he nor his friends is good at playing basketball. ◯

   _____

2. Either you or Jack have to pay for the broken window. ◯

   _____

3. Either Peter or his brothers decide who gets to use the computer first. ◯

   _____

4. Neither Wendy nor her sisters knows how to drive. ◯

   _____

5. Either my friends or I are going to prepare snacks for the outing. ◯

   _____

My Notes

   _____

   _____

   _____

   _____

UNIT 7

Conditional Clauses

A **conditional clause** begins with "if" and talks about a possible situation and its results. When the conditional clause comes before the main clause, it is followed by a comma.

There are four types of conditional sentences.

Zero Conditional Sentences:

- for general truths
- conditional clause: simple present tense
- main clause: simple present tense

Example

conditional clause   main clause
If the dog <u>barks</u>,/it probably <u>senses</u> something unusual.

A.   Complete the zero conditional sentences with the correct clauses.

all cars stop	there is no school
if it rains	if he has given it to you
it turns to ice	if we are tired or sick
they are ready to eat	if my alarm clock does not work

1.   If you put water in the freezer, _____ .

2.   We need to rest _____ .

3.   If it is Sunday, _____ .

4.   If the avocados are soft, _____ .

5.   If the light turns red, _____ .

6.   Tell her not to go _____ .

7.   Mom, please wake me up _____

   _____ .

8.   The bike belongs to you _____ .

First Conditional Sentences:

- for situations that are likely to happen
- conditional clause: simple present tense
- main clause: simple future tense

Example

If you <u>practise</u> every day, you <u>will win</u> the competition.

B. Circle the correct forms of the verbs to complete the conditional sentences.

1. If Cecilia **is / will be** willing to go the extra mile for this company, she **stands / will stand** a good chance of landing the job.

2. I **make / will make** good use of it if you **give / will give** it to me.

3. No one **finds / will find** out if you **keep / will keep** it a secret.

4. If we both **agree / will agree** to go ahead with the task immediately, we **are / will be** able to complete it on schedule.

5. If Terence **travels / will travel** to China, he **goes / will go** to Beijing first.

6. Nellie **achieves / will achieve** her goals if she **works / will work** hard enough.

7. If you **are / will be** thankful for everything, you **are / will be** happy.

8. If it **rains / will rain** , we **cancel / will cancel** the game.

C. Complete the conditional sentences to tell about something likely to happen.

1. If I do all my chores, _____ .

2. If you forgive your friend, _____ .

3. Adrian will not go to the party _____ .

4. You will be sad _____ .

Second Conditional Sentences:

- for situations that are very unlikely to happen or for unrealistic situations
- conditional clause: simple past tense
- main clause: has a modal verb ("could" or "would")

Examples

- If I <u>had</u> wings, I <u>could fly</u> to wherever I like.
- Sharon <u>would make</u> me a gingerbread house if she <u>baked</u>.

D.   Write conditional sentences to tell about something unlikely to happen using the given clauses. Use the appropriate tenses in the clauses.

1.   Devon comes. He brings his pet dog with him.

_____

2.   They invite you. You are a committee member.

_____

3.   We are denied entry. We have our gathering somewhere else.

_____

4.   I am the teacher. I teach my students how to make telescopes.

_____

5.   Max makes a candy castle. He has millions of candies.

_____

6.   Jen stays at the party. Fran is very happy.

_____

7.   Karen saves the planet. She has superpowers.

_____

_____

8.   I own a spaceship. I fly to other planets.

_____

_____

Third Conditional Sentences:

- for situations that could have happened in the past but did not
- conditional clause: past perfect tense
- main clause:

  "would/could/should have" + past participle

Examples

- If I <u>had known</u> the truth, I <u>would have told</u> you.
- If Peter <u>had run</u> faster, he <u>would have won</u> the race.

E. Rewrite the conditional sentences so that they are correct.

1. The team would have lost if Derek did not hit a homerun in the ninth inning.

   _____

2. We would have stopped if he would have warned us.

   _____

3. If Rachel had been more supportive, the team had been able to make it.

   _____

4. If Dad had shown them the pass, he had not have been charged.

   _____

5. If the gate had been locked, the animals had not run away.

   _____

   _____

My Notes

_____

_____

_____

_____

UNIT 8

Dependent Clauses as Nouns, Adjectives, and Adverbs

A **dependent clause** cannot stand alone as a sentence. It has to be attached to an independent clause and adds more information to that clause.

A **noun clause** functions as a noun in a sentence. It can act as the subject or the object of a verb, or the object of a preposition. It answers the question "Who(m)?" or "What?".

Examples

Noun Clauses:

- <u>Whatever you choose to do</u> is fine with us. subject of a verb

- I think <u>that Lucy is reliable</u>. object of a verb

- You can give the book to <u>whomever you prefer</u>. object of a preposition

---

A. **Underline the noun clauses in the sentences. Then identify them as the subject of a verb (S), the object of a verb (O), or the object of a preposition (OP).**

1. He realized that he needed his parents' permission before going on a vacation with his friends. (   )

2. Whatever you do has to be both sensible and meaningful. (   )

3. Whether or not they could make it remained to be seen. (   )

4. Where the robbers are hiding is still unknown. (   )

5. They did not know which train passed by the little town. (   )

6. The tourists were uncertain about how they would get to the city. (   )

7. I am fine with whichever movie you pick. (   )

8. The medal will be given to whoever comes first in the race. (   )

An **adjective clause** acts like an adjective and modifies a noun or pronoun. It answers questions like "Which?" or "What kind of?".

In formal writing, an adjective clause begins with a relative pronoun like "who", "that", or "which". In informal writing, the relative pronoun is often left out.

Examples

- In formal writing:

  Jenny loved the bag <u>that her mom bought for her</u>.

- In informal writing:

  Jenny loved the bag <u>her mom bought for her</u>.

B. Put the adjective clauses in the sentences in parentheses.

1. The man whom I met today is Sam's dad.

2. The seafood dinner that we had last night was delicious.

3. That is the store where I bought my new shoes from.

4. My favourite sweater is the one that my grandma knitted for me.

5. Jeff was looking for the book that Jenny recommended him to read.

6. The glass, which Tracy accidentally dropped, shattered to pieces.

C. Rewrite each of the sentences by adding an adjective clause.

1. The house looked run-down.

   Formal _____

2. The article was well-written.

   Formal _____

3. Have you seen the painting?

   Informal _____

4. He claimed the prize.

   Informal _____

An **adverb clause** functions like an adverb in a main clause. It answers questions like "When?", "Why?", or "How?". It usually begins with a subordinating conjunction like "because", "when", "where", "since", "after", or "so that".

Examples

- He built a house <u>where the old church used to stand</u>.
- <u>While I was asleep,</u> the phone rang.

D. **Check if the underlined clause is an adverb clause. Otherwise, put a cross.**

1. It was too late <u>when his friend arrived at the movie theatre</u>. ◯

2. We stayed out <u>until the sun set</u>. ◯

3. They stopped what they were doing <u>so that they could watch the news</u>. ◯

4. Do you know <u>what Martha ordered</u>? ◯

5. <u>Since it rained</u>, we stayed in and played board games. ◯

6. The place <u>where we went for a picnic yesterday</u> is beautiful. ◯

E. **Rewrite each sentence by adding an adverb clause with the subordinating conjunction in parentheses.**

1. I cannot be late. (because)

   _____

2. The cat knocked over a plant. (while)

   _____

3. She won the race. (after)

   _____

4. Mika tidied her room. (so that)

   _____

5. He was baking cookies. (when)

   _____

F. **Underline the noun, adjective, and adverb clauses in the sentences. Then write their sentence numbers in the correct boxes to show their types.**

1. He put a mark where he thought the treasure was buried.

2. Everyone found it hard to believe that he knew the code.

3. Whichever road you take is your own choice.

4. The player who scored the winning run is my brother.

5. It is important to reflect on how we can improve ourselves as individuals.

6. The lady whose hat was red threw a loonie into the water fountain.

7. It started raining before the soccer game could even begin.

8. We drove down the highway until we could see the first ray of the morning sun.

9. David has always been a reliable friend whom everyone can trust.

10. The Watsons did not go on the trip because some of their family friends came to visit them.

11. What Ken wants to know is how he can join the basketball team.

12. Kate showed me the dress that she wished to get in the magazine.

— Noun Clause —	— Adjective Clause —	— Adverb Clause —

My Notes

_____

_____

_____

_____

UNIT

9 Inversion

Inversion is when the normal word order of a sentence is reversed. Instead of the verb going after the subject, the subject goes after the verb.

One of the most common uses of inversion is to form questions. If the sentence has an auxiliary verb, it is reversed with the subject to form a question.

Examples

• <u>You are</u> sad.
  subject verb

  → Are you sad?

• <u>Julia is leaving</u>.
  subject   main verb

  auxiliary verb

  → Is Julia leaving?

A.   Change the sentences to questions using inversion.

1. He was able to catch the last train.

    _____ to catch the last train?

2. They were going to the park before he came.

    _____ to the park before he came?

3. Ella has been volunteering quite often these days.

    _____ quite often these days?

4. Grandpa and Grandma will visit us this summer.

    _____ us this summer?

5. Benny can take care of your dog while you are away.

    _____ care of your dog while you are away?

6. Neelu and Jessie are neighbours.

    _____ neighbours?

7. Jessica will be going to buy some eggs.

    _____ to buy some eggs?

Inversion is also used to add emphasis in a sentence. When a sentence begins with a negative adverb or adverb phrase, the subject and the verb are inverted.

Negative Adverbs and Adverb Phrases: hardly, never, seldom, rarely, scarcely, little, in no way, on no account

Examples

- I have seldom heard such bickering.

  Seldom <u>have I</u> heard such bickering.

- You should not do anything irrational on any account.

  On no account <u>should you</u> do anything irrational.

B.   Check the correctly inverted sentences.

1.   I have seldom felt so helpless.

(A)   Seldom have felt I so helpless.

(B)   Seldom have I felt so helpless.

2.   He did not realize the magnitude of the problem.

(A)   Little did he realize the magnitude of the problem.

(B)   Little did realize he the magnitude of the problem.

3.   We have never seen an ocean so blue.

(A)   Never have we seen an ocean so blue.

(B)   Never we have seen an ocean so blue.

4.   They rarely dine at that restaurant.

(A)   Rarely dine they at that restaurant.

(B)   Rarely do they dine at that restaurant.

5.   We did not expect to be able to sweep the champion team.

(A)   Hardly we did expect to be able to sweep the champion team.

(B)   Hardly did we expect to be able to sweep the champion team.

6.   Eli does not know that it was Jason who helped him.

(A)   In no way does Eli know that it was Jason who helped him.

(B)   In no way Eli does know that it was Jason who helped him.

Inversion can also be used in a conditional sentence if the conditional clause contains "had", "were", or "should".

Example

If I had known you broke your favourite mug, I would have bought you a new one.

<u>Had I known</u> you broke your favourite mug, I would have bought you a new one.

C.   Rewrite the conditional sentences using inversion.

1.   If Lizzie were taller, she would be allowed on the roller coaster.

Were _____

_____ .

2.   If they had bought the tickets earlier, they would have saved some money.

Had _____ .

3.   If you should require more details, please visit our website.

Should _____ .

4.   If we had practised more together, we would have won the game.

_____

5.   If you should want to participate in the event, please sign up by the end of June.

_____

6.   If Jenna had been correct, we would all have received a surprise gift.

_____

7.   If Harry were the chairperson, he would definitely turn down the proposal.

_____

8.   If Mrs. Clark were to run the marathon, we would all run with her.

_____

Inversion can also be used after the words "here" and "there" when they are used as adverbs of place.

I opened the box and <u>there stood</u> the figurine I had wished to get.

D. **Look at the pictures. Write sentences of your own using inversion with "here" or "there".**

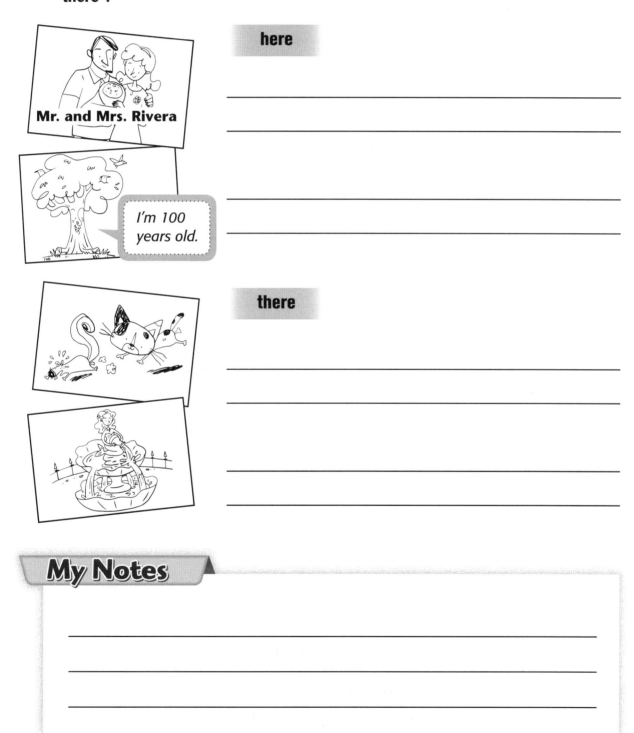

here

_____

_____

_____

_____

there

_____

_____

_____

_____

My Notes

_____

_____

_____

_____

UNIT 10 Voice and Mood

Verbs in the **active voice** show the action of the subject. Verbs in the **passive voice** show something else acting on the subject. While the active voice is more forceful and should be used whenever possible, the passive voice provides a shift of emphasis – from the doer of the action to the thing or person being acted upon.

Note that in using the passive voice, the doer is sometimes left out so that the reader's attention is further directed at the person or thing being acted upon.

Examples

Active Voice:

• We ate ten pizzas!

Passive Voice:

• Ten pizzas were eaten by us!

Passive Voice without the Doer of the Action:

• Ten pizzas were eaten!

A. Rewrite the sentences using the passive voice.

You may leave out the "doer" of the action if it does not affect the clarity of the sentence.

1. The firefighters put out the fire in less than an hour.

   _____

   _____

2. We will hold the annual meeting as scheduled.

   _____

   _____

3. They saw a baby whale off the shore.

   _____

4. The teacher handed out the pamphlets to all the Grade 8 students.

   _____

5. We should return all borrowed books to the library before noon today.

   _____

6. The principal awarded Janet The Student of the Year Award.

   _____

B. Write in the boxes to indicate whether the underlined parts are in the active voice (A) or passive voice (P). Then write the numbers of the passive voice parts and rewrite them in the active voice.

Dodge ball is a fun game enjoyed by grade school children. [1.] There are many ways of playing it. A popular way is to divide the players into two teams. The players on one team stay inside a circle on the ground [2.] and those on the other team stand around outside it. A big, rubber ball is thrown and aimed at the players inside the circle. [3.] The players inside may run around whenever they need to dodge the ball [4.] as long as they stay within the circle. The ball can only be thrown [5.] to hit the players below the waist. If the ball is thrown [6.] and hits someone above the waist, the thrower has to leave the game. [7.] If a player in the circle is hit, [8.] he or she becomes one of the players outside the circle. The game ends when only one person remains inside the circle. [9.]

Rewritten in the Active Voice

☐ _____

_____

☐ _____

_____

☐ _____

☐ _____

☐ _____

Section 2

Grammar

There are three types of **mood**: indicative, imperative, and subjunctive.

The **indicative mood** is used to make a statement or ask a question.

The **imperative mood** is used to express a command or a request.

Examples

Indicative Mood:
- The teacher will arrive soon.
- Where is the library?

Imperative Mood:
- Please let me know by noon today.

C.   Read the sentences. Circle "IND" for indicative mood and "IMP" for imperative mood.

1.   They are still awaiting the medical report.   **IND / IMP**

2.   Tell Susan that her mother called her just now.   **IND / IMP**

3.   Should I go and seek advice from Mr. Walton?   **IND / IMP**

4.   Make sure that each of them is given a bonus pack.   **IND / IMP**

5.   Ms. Lee wanted to make sure that everything was in order.   **IND / IMP**

6.   We can tell if Keith is lying by looking at his posture.   **IND / IMP**

D.   Change the mood of the sentences to imperative.

1.   You must not waste any more time on the minor details.

_____

2.   I would appreciate it if you could contact Mrs. Jones on my behalf.

_____

3.   You may choose to buy it online if you want to save time.

_____

4.   You should bear right when you see the sign "Snowview".

_____

_____

The **subjunctive mood** is used to express wishes or hypothetical situations.

Note that "were" instead of "was" is used in the if-clause even if the subject is singular. Also, the past perfect tense is used to denote a hypothetical case.

Examples

Subjunctive Mood:

- I wish he were here to help.

- If he had helped me, I would have been able to meet the deadline.

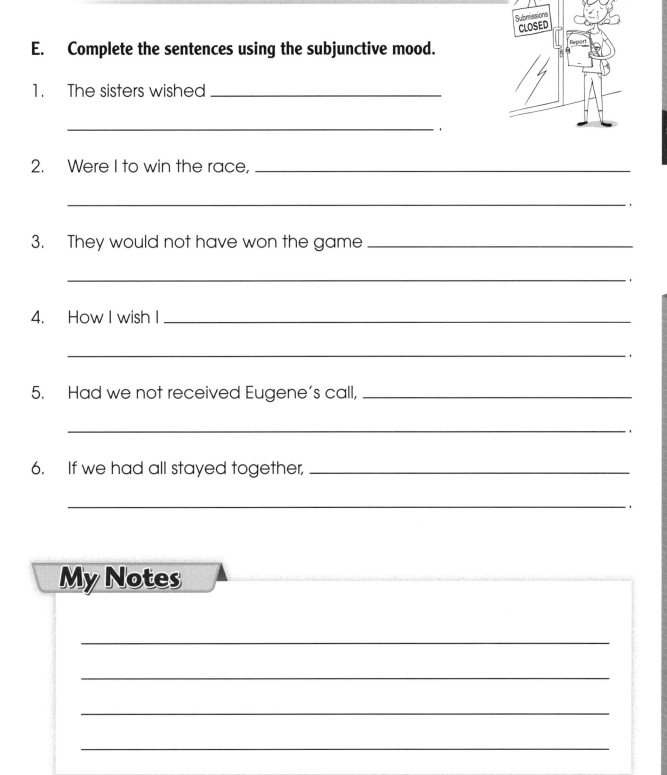

E. **Complete the sentences using the subjunctive mood.**

1. The sisters wished _____

   _____ .

2. Were I to win the race, _____

   _____ .

3. They would not have won the game _____

   _____ .

4. How I wish I _____

   _____ .

5. Had we not received Eugene's call, _____

   _____ .

6. If we had all stayed together, _____

   _____ .

My Notes

_____

_____

_____

_____

UNIT

11 Ellipses and Dashes

An **ellipsis** is a punctuation mark characterized by a set of three dots.

An ellipsis is used to:

- omit a quoted word, phrase, clause, or paragraph.
- omit unnecessary information.
- show a pause in a narrative.
- show someone trailing off in thought in a narrative.

Examples

- She woke up, got dressed, ate breakfast, and left for work.
  She woke up...and left for work.

- Derek could not make up his mind on what to do...Get help?...Try again?...Give up?

- Ada said, "This seems to be the only solution but..."

A. Rewrite the sentences using ellipses where appropriate.

1. There was a flash of lightning and then suddenly there was thunder.

   _____

2. I was going to leave but at that moment, I heard a strange noise.

   _____

3. Josh went to the store to buy apples, oranges, lettuce, tomatoes, cheese, and milk, and came back with two bags of groceries.

   _____

4. Stella dreamily sighed, "I wish I were a princess."

   _____

5. The committee, established in 2000 and has since then presented the Outstanding Service Award annually, is proud to present the award to Jacob Stubbs.

   _____

6. Anna walked in, turned on the light, and screamed as everyone cried, "Surprise!"

   _____

A **dash** can be used to:

- set off an appositive or an explanation to further the reader's understanding of a sentence.

- add emphasis.

Tom   Alan

B. **Rewrite the sentences using dashes where appropriate. Make any other necessary changes.**

1. I will eat broccoli so long as it is covered in cheese.

   _____

   _____

2. She ran to the park or rather she leaped to the park.

   _____

3. There are only three things Tim is afraid of. They are thunder, heights, and loneliness.

   _____

4. All four girls made the honours list. The four girls were Jenna, Marilyn, Rebecca, and Kristina.

   _____

5. He would only leave his house during the winter for one thing, that is, pizza.

   _____

6. My brother hates country music. He also hates rock music and he would never go line dancing.

   _____

7. Ruby called Dr. Crowley on Monday to schedule an appointment. Dr. Crowley is her family doctor.

   _____

C. **Add ellipses and dashes to the sentences with a ∧ . Cross out the words to be omitted for ellipses if needed.**

1. Samuel Langhorne Clemens was a famous American writer better known by his pen name Mark Twain.

2. Mark Twain has written "The Adventures of Tom Sawyer", "Adventures of Huckleberry Finn", "Life on the Mississippi", "The Prince and the Pauper", and "A Tramp Abroad" and is often referred to as the father of American literature.

3. When Twain was four, his family moved to Hannibal (a port town on the Mississippi River) where he was inspired to write "Adventures of Huckleberry Finn".

4. Ernest Hemingway another famous American writer is best known for his novel "The Old Man and the Sea".

5. In 1920, Hemingway took a job at a newspaper in Toronto the Toronto Star.

6. Many critics touted Hemingway's "A Clean, Well-lighted Place" a short story as one of the best stories ever written.

7. To be a good writer (I have concluded after interviewing 12 writers) is to write clearly and concisely.

8. I have a wish to be as great and successful as the famous Mark Twain and Ernest Hemingway one day.

D. Write sentences using ellipses and dashes to continue the prompts.

1. There is something strange outside my window.

   _____

   _____

   _____

2. The road ahead is obscured by a thick fog.

   _____

   _____

   _____

3. I waited for the culprit to return to the scene of the crime.

   _____

   _____

   _____

4. The statue has stood there for over a hundred years.

   _____

   _____

   _____

5. No one knows who has left the kitten in front of the store.

   _____

   _____

   _____

My Notes

   _____

   _____

   _____

   _____

A.   Circle the answers.

1.   Which sentence contains a prepositional verb?

I work out with you.

I depend on you.

I can't keep up with you.

2.   Which is a characteristic of a finite verb?

It is not the main verb in the sentence.

It agrees with the subject in number.

It does not agree with the subject in number.

3.   The underlined verb in this sentence is a/an _____ .

Riding requires great skills.

participle

infinitive

gerund

4.   Which group contains only non-progressive verbs?

feel, see, smell, believe

feel, drive, smell, love

feel, be, teach, want

5.   What do these non-progressive verbs indicate?

belong, own, have

mental states

existence

possession

6.   A/An _____ is used to express permission, ability, and more.

modal verb

correlative conjunction

inverted sentence

7.   Which question with a modal verb is formed from this sentence by inversion?

I may borrow your car.

May I borrow your car?

Could I borrow your car?

Should I borrow your car?

8.   Which sentence shows the correct order of adjectives?

My wooden brown chair broke.

The wise old English teacher smiled.

I got a red new fishing rod.

9.   Which pair of words contains an adjective with its correct function?

cotton – material

ancient – origin

red – purpose

10.   Which correlative conjunction shows one of the options in a sentence?

not only...but also

neither...nor

either...or

11. Which sentence has the correct pronoun-antecedent agreement?

Either you or your friends knows the answer.

Neither Julia nor Robert knew where his money was.

Neither Tim nor the twins brought his books.

12. Which is a characteristic of a zero conditional sentence?

It is used for situations that are likely to happen.

It is used for situations that could have happened but did not.

It is used for general truths.

13. Which type of sentence is this?

If you had told me, I would have known.

first conditional sentence

second conditional sentence

third conditional sentence

14. Which sentence contains a noun clause?

I like the dress that you gave me.

You cannot donate it to whomever you choose.

The bell rang after I went to bed.

15. Which sentence uses inversion correctly to add emphasis?

Rarely do I go out anymore.

I rarely go out anymore.

Rarely I do go out anymore.

16. Which sentence uses inversion correctly for this conditional sentence?

If you had been there, you would have laughed.

Had you not been there, you would laugh.

Had you laughed, you would have been there.

Had you been there, you would have laughed.

17. Which sentence is in the indicative mood?

Write to your aunt now.

They could not wait for their turn.

Remember to lock the door.

18. Which can be used to set off an appositive?

Types of Verbs

B.   Write "prepositional", "phrasal", "finite", "non-finite", or "non-progressive" to identify each group of verbs. Then fill in the blanks with the correct verbs.

Types of Verbs

a._____	b._____	c._____	d._____	e._____
shut down set out read over	listening weighed given	realized have want	believe in approve of	to learn to progress challenging inspiring

The year was 2050 and the world had changed. Technology had allowed

society to flourish and the government had 1._____ to equip each

student with great knowledge. "It is time 2._____ as much as

possible," the familiar voice of the artificial intelligence system rang out. "We,

the Ministry of Education, have 3._____ that schools are no longer

viable. Therefore, public schools will be 4._____ effective July 1.

Students are 5._____ the agreed upon curriculum which will be

programmed into them. Every household will be 6._____ one of our

7._____ information packages next Friday to 8._____ . As

always, we 9._____ you."

Three students from Tech High were attentively 10._____ to the

announcement after a 11._____ game of soccer. "This means no more

school!" said Susan. "I don't 12._____ to go to school anyway." Dorian

quickly chimed in, "Yeah! We will already 13._____ all the knowledge we

need." Julian, however, had been quiet as he 14._____ the implications

of such a drastic decision. He knew he could not 15._____ it.

Order of Adjectives and Correlative Conjunctions

C. **Write the correct order of adjectives above the underlined adjectives if needed. Then fill in the blanks with the correct correlative conjunctions.**

The following Friday, the streets stirred with voices as <u>state-of-the-art information</u> packages were handed out to the parents of <u>school-going, young</u> children. This was met with a mixed reaction.

Some parents were 1._____ glad that their children would be well-learned 2._____ glad that they would not have to drive them to and from school. Also, they thought this meant spending less time and money on school projects. Instead, they could focus on their work and their children might even like it better. Others, however, were alarmed at the idea but they did not know who to turn to and feared that they might never be heard.

3._____ had the townspeople gathered to voice their opinion 4._____ government-employed robots proceeded to program chips into students. Soon, <u>educational well-established</u> institutions were shut down – buildings that were once full of laughter turned into <u>deserted, huge</u> ghost towns. 5._____ were the schools empty 6._____ the streets were 7._____ abandoned as people started staying in their homes, sheltered and isolated...existing but not really living.

Meanwhile, Julian, who was supposed to attend high school in the fall, refused to be programmed with the knowledge chip. He read 8._____ <u>old, worn-out</u> books 9._____ he could and accessed online libraries to learn as much as possible on his own.

However, the government had been alerted that Julian had not activated his <u>knowledge personal</u> chip. And so, he was asked to go down to City Hall with his parents and explain himself.

Conditional Sentences and Dependent Clauses

D.   Write the numbers of the underlined sentences and clauses in the correct boxes.

1. If Julian had been scared, he would have asked his parents to speak on his behalf. But he was determined to do it all on his own. He was determined to plead his case, to have his voice heard, and to save his beloved school, 2. which the government had shut down.

3. *If they ask me for supporting evidence, I will not have enough information to prove my case*, Julian thought as he prepared for the meeting. As he had not activated his knowledge chip, he had to find information on his own. So he decided to conduct surveys himself. One of the most important questions his survey included was 4. "If you had an option, what would you choose: the knowledge chip or going back to school?" He also asked some grown-ups if they agreed with the government not allowing their children to learn independently and think for themselves. After researching and preparing tirelessly for about a month, Julian knew that he had done his best. 5. *Whatever the government decides* will be acceptable to me, he reasoned with himself.

On the day of the meeting, Julian picked up the notes 6. that he had worked so hard on and went to City Hall. He was surprised to see that his friends Susan and Dorian were also there. 7. While he delivered a moving speech, his friends cheered him on. Although he was one of the very few students who had not activated his knowledge chip, he was supported by many. His opinion was acknowledged and heard by a silent room full of parents, students, government officials, and educators.

8. As he concluded, he looked around expectantly to weigh their expressions and eagerly awaited the verdict.

Type of Conditional Sentence

First Conditional Sentence: ☐

Second Conditional Sentence: ☐

Third Conditional Sentence: ☐

Dependent Clause as...

Noun: ☐

Adverb: ☐ ☐

Adjective: ☐ ☐

Inversion, Voice, Ellipses, and Dashes

E. Check the correctly inverted sentences.

1. "I have never heard such a passionate speech," said the Minister of Education.

    (A) "Never have I heard such a passionate speech," said the Minister of Education.

    (B) "Never I have heard such a passionate speech," said the Minister of Education.

2. The government did not foresee the impacts of the knowledge chip.

    (A) Little the impacts were of the knowledge chip foreseen.

    (B) Little did the government foresee the impacts of the knowledge chip.

3. "You are ready for schools to open again," said the governor.

    (A) "Are you ready for schools to open again?" asked the governor.

    (B) "Ready are you for schools to open again?" asked the governor.

F. Write "Active Voice" or "Passive Voice" above the underlined sentences. Then add ellipses or dashes in the circles.

Before the governor could say another word, <u>voices of agreement rose up throughout the hall</u>. <u>Julian's wise words had caused a massive uproar and the listeners were moved by his impassioned speech</u>.

After hours of deliberation ◯ much of which were spent by an apprehensive Julian sitting on the edge of his seat ◯ the governor finally came to the decision that the boy who had voiced his opinion was ◯ right!

The governor went on to elaborate that although technology was powerful, it could not replace social interaction and individual learning. <u>Traditional education could not be replaced by knowledge chips</u>.

That fall, knowledge chips were recalled as schools reopened. Julian smiled to himself as he walked through the doors of his bustling new high school.

Section 3

Reading

UNIT 1 Harry's Dream

It was the first day of school and Harry was walking past the auditorium when he saw a poster for a casting call. It was for the school's annual play that would be held at the end of the year. Harry had always wanted to act but it was more "popular" to play basketball. However, when he saw the sign, he secretly wished that one day he could act.

When Harry told his basketball friends about his wish, they all laughed and brushed him off. They thought it was silly that Harry, the star basketball player, would want to switch to acting. Without his friends' encouragement, Harry felt defeated.

When Harry told his father that he wanted to try out for the school play, his

father also laughed at his dream. His father told him, "Why would you want to act when you are so talented at basketball?" Harry was saddened by his father's response. Without his father's or his friends' encouragement, Harry did not feel confident enough to try out for the play.

The next day at school, the drama teacher, Mr. Peare, caught Harry looking wishfully at the casting call sign. Mr. Peare told him, "Harry, I think you should audition." However, Harry told him that he could not because his father and his friends did not think that he should pursue acting. Mr. Peare reassured him, "Harry, you should do what you think is right for you, regardless of what anyone else says. Think about it." Harry took what Mr. Peare said to heart. That night, he could not sleep. *If I want to pursue acting, I should do it. Why can't I do both basketball and acting?* he thought.

A few days later, Harry decided to audition for the school play in secret. He got the lead role! As excited as he was, he did not tell anyone about this because he was not sure how his father and friends would react to seeing him in the school play. Also, he wanted to focus on the rehearsals without worrying about explaining himself.

Finally, it was opening night and everyone had come to watch. Harry's father and friends could not find Harry anywhere in the auditorium. To their surprise, they saw him on stage! When the play ended, Harry's father and friends gave the loudest applause to show how proud they were of him.

After the play, Harry's father told him, "Son, I should not have doubted you. If you want to act and play basketball, I support you." Harry's friends chimed in, "We support you too, Harry." Then they lifted Harry on their shoulders and chanted, "Harry! Harry! Harry!".

I must be the luckiest guy in the world, Harry thought. Mr. Peare's advice had worked and Harry was happy to celebrate with his father and friends.

> The protagonist of a story is the leading character. The antagonist is the character who opposes the protagonist.

A. Circle the answers.

1. Who is the protagonist?

   Mr. Peare

   Harry's father

   Harry

2. Who are the antagonists?

   Harry's dad and Mr. Peare

   Harry's dad and friends

   Mr. Peare and the school

3. What is Harry's dream?

   to play basketball

   to act

   to be a drama teacher

4. When is the school play held?

   at the beginning of the year

   in the middle of the year

   at the end of the year

5. How did Harry know about the casting call?

   Mr. Peare told him.

   There was a rumour at school.

   He saw a poster for a casting call.

6. Who is Mr. Peare?

   the basketball coach

   the drama teacher

   the school play's lead actor

7. How does Harry feel about getting the lead role in the school play?

   excited

   nervous

   scared

B.   Answer the questions.

1.   What is the message of the short story?

_____

_____

2.   Explain the type of conflict Harry faces.

_____

_____

_____

_____

3.   Do you think Mr. Peare is an important character in the story? Why or why not?

_____

_____

There are four types of conflict:

1. Physical
   character versus character

2. Environmental
   character versus nature

3. Social
   character versus society

4. Psychological
   character versus self

C.   Write the letters to identify the elements of the plot diagram for the short story "Harry's Dream".

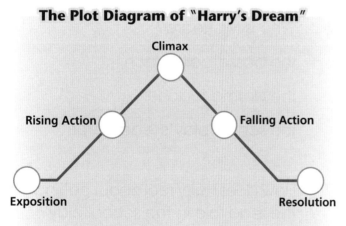

The Plot Diagram of "Harry's Dream"

Climax

Rising Action   Falling Action

Exposition   Resolution

Exposition:	introduces characters and setting
Rising Action:	reveals and intensifies conflict
Climax:	the turning point of the story
Falling Action:	events leading toward the resolution
Resolution:	shows the outcome of the conflict

Ⓐ Harry feels defeated and saddened by the lack of support from his father and friends.

Ⓑ Harry feels happy to attain the support of his father and friends.

Ⓒ Harry sees a poster for a casting call on the first day of school.

Ⓓ Harry follows Mr. Peare's advice and decides to secretly pursue acting.

Ⓔ Harry's father and friends watch his performance in the play.

D. Read the alternative ending to "Harry's Dream" and compare and contrast it to the original ending of the story.

Alternative Ending

When the play ended, Harry's father and friends approached him.

Harry's father told him, "Son, you were great in the play, but I don't want you to pursue acting. It will take too much time away from basketball." Harry's friends agreed. "Yeah, Harry, just stick with basketball," one of them said.

Although Harry was troubled by their lack of support, he was determined to follow his dreams. He hoped that one day, they would think differently. For now, he was content.

Ask Yourself

- What are the similarities and differences between the two endings?

- Which ending hints at what would happen next?

- Which ending gives the story a proper resolution?

- Which ending effectively shows the moral of the story?

Similarity

Difference

My Notes

_____

_____

_____

_____

UNIT 2 Two Kingdoms

ACT 1, Prologue

Two kingdoms steeped in controversy,
Both of them strong in might.
They have forgotten the art of mercy,
And showing none, all they do is fight.
Brutish battles destroy all livelihood;
Prosperity is now a thing of the past,
Estranged from the land for good,
Unless peace can be made at last.
One boy will emerge with this very dream,
And to make the fighting end he will scheme.
But alone in his wish for peace he will not be.
A girl on the other side schemes the same as he.

ACT 1, Scene 1

It is late at night. Sounds of fighting, thunder, and rain can be heard in the distance. Tom, the boy, is alone in his room. He is pacing back and forth.

TOM: There must be a way to end this pointless conflict! I should speak with the other king and try to reach an agreement. But what if I am captured? I cannot shake this foreboding feeling that something terrible will happen to me there. Even the weather is ominous! The wind, howling like a pack of wolves, torments me. I cannot even hear the angry sounds of battle out there in the fields. And...wait, what's that? The lightning illuminates Father's sword as if it were commanding me to use it. Its sinister gleam is almost blinding. Surely, this must be a sign of things to come. But of good or bad things, I cannot yet say.

(Tom's friend, Jim, enters the room.)

JIM: You've locked yourself away in your room all evening. We need you on the battlefield!

(Tom says nothing and continues to look upon the battle.)

JIM: What's wrong? I've never seen you look this troubled before.

TOM: Jim, I know we should be brave and continue fighting...but look how much our kingdom has lost! *(He points at the battlefield.)* Day after day, we head to the battlefield and come back more worn and injured than before. The cattle have been frightened off by the sounds of battle. This storm, raging like a wild beast, has drowned all the crops and our people are starving. This ominous weather breeds sickness! I long for the days of peace and prosperity, when children can go out and play on the streets without fear. *(He pause.)* No, I can no longer be indecisive and do nothing! I will leave at sunrise to visit the other king and request a peace treaty to end this fighting once and for all!

(Tom paces out of the room as Jim follows him.)

End of ACT 1, Scene 1

A. Circle the answers.

1. The two kingdoms are _____ .

   strong and merciful

   strong but ruthless

   strong and prosperous

2. What is the setting of Act 1, Scene 1?

   in the morning in Tom's room

   in the morning in Jim's room

   at night in Tom's room

3. The main characters in Act 1, Scene 1 are _____ .

   Tom and his friend Jim

   Jim and a girl in the other kingdom

   a girl and the king of the other kingdom

4. How is the weather?

   calm

   cloudy

   stormy

5. What does Tom see when the lightning flashes?

   his father

   his father's sword

   a sign on his father's sword

6. What has frightened off the cattle?

   the sounds of battle

   the sounds of thunder

   the ominous weather

7. When will Tom leave?

   right away

   in the morning

   in the afternoon

8. What is Tom's plan?

   to speak to the king of the other kingdom

   to fight with his father's sword

   to find the girl in the other kingdom

Reading

B.   Answer the questions.

1.   What can you tell about Tom's character? Give two examples from the text to explain.

_____

_____

_____

2.   Describe the condition of Tom's kingdom.

_____

_____

_____

3.

> *How does Tom feel about visiting the king of the other kingdom? Explain.*

_____

_____

_____

C.   Check the correct points about the prologue of "Two Kingdoms".

A prologue is an introduction to a play. It is addressed to the audience at the opening of the play and establishes context for the plot.

The Prologue...

○   is written in poetic form.

○   is written in prose.

○   follows a rhyme scheme.

○   introduces all the characters.

○   tells us that the play is about two opposing kingdoms.

○   tells us that Tom alone will stop the fighting.

D. **Read Tom's soliloquy and check the elements it contains. Then answer the questions.**

There must be a way to end this pointless conflict! I should speak with the other king and try to reach an agreement. But what if I am captured? I cannot shake this foreboding feeling that something terrible will happen to me there. Even the weather is ominous!...And...wait, what's that? The lightning illuminates Father's sword as if it were commanding me to use it. Its sinister gleam is almost blinding. Surely, this must be a sign of things to come. But of good or bad things, I cannot say.

Tom

A soliloquy is a character's speech to himself or herself, expressing his or her thoughts and feelings aloud.

Foreshadowing is used to indicate future events to the audience.

Elements of Tom's Soliloquy

○ simile

○ metaphor

○ foreshadowing

○ stage direction

○ dialogue

○ clear objective

○ one speaker

1. What does the soliloquy show about Tom's feelings?

_____

_____

2. Do you think the soliloquy foreshadows something good or bad? Why?

_____

_____

_____

My Notes

_____

_____

_____

_____

UNIT

3 Junk Food Is Good Food

THE POST

Volume 1, Issue 2   SATIRE NEWS AND OPINIONS   July 7, 2019

JUNK FOOD IS GOOD FOOD

By Lialiar Pansonfire

A new study has been done by junk food enthusiasts which concludes that eating excessive amounts of fatty, sugary, and oily junk food is indeed healthful for you after all. After hours of gathering thorough data from a handful of random, anonymous online sources with no credibility, enthusiasts have discovered a special nutrient called "junk" – which they claim is exclusively found in junk food and supposedly helps in brain development.

The Faculty of Advanced Kitchen Eating

Dr. Sill Ypants at the Faculty of Advanced Kitchen Eating (F.A.K.E.) said he was astonished to hear of this remarkable discovery by self-proclaimed junk food experts. "These enthusiasts may not be real doctors," he stated, "but as a fellow lover of good, greasy food, I can say this discovery is a true scientific breakthrough...without all the actual science, of course."

The "discovery" was first made when Mr. Swee Tuuth, head of the Junk Obsessed Kitchen Eatery (J.O.K.E.), realized that whenever he ate junk food, he could feel his neurons spark up and his intelligence enhance to a higher level. When asked if he was merely experiencing a common sugar rush, Mr. Tuuth declined to comment. Nonetheless, he published his observations on online forums and found that other people had similar findings. Seeing nothing wrong with citing the opinions of uninformed strangers on the Internet as fact, Mr. Tuuth then concluded that junk food did indeed contain a special nutrient to help improve intelligence.

The nutritional make-up of the "junk" nutrient is said to be complex. Due to the abundance of toxins, fatty acids, and external chemicals present in our organs when we eat junk food, the nutrient itself is apparently difficult to uncover. However, F.A.K.E. doctors insist that the nutrient "has got to be buried somewhere beneath all those nasty toxins", which they assert are a key part of the nutrient's composition.

Dr. Sill Ypants has gone on the record to call for the implementation of junk food in all health service buildings across the nation. "We really should be replacing water with soda and vegetables with sugary desserts for the good of our future generations. F.A.K.E. doctors like me know that junk food is the path to good health." When asked if his team at F.A.K.E. could supply us with an approximated illustration of the chemical structure of the nutrient "junk", Dr. Sill Ypants merely said that studying the supposed nutrient was "not a priority at this time".

A.   Circle the answers.

1.   It is claimed that the "junk" nutrient helps develop _____ .

the sugar level

the brain

good eating habits

2.   Which group is Dr. Sill Ypants a part of?

F.A.K.E.

J.O.K.E.

an online forum

3.   What does F.A.K.E. stand for?

Factory of Advanced Kitchen Eating

Faculty of Advanced Kitchen Eatery

Faculty of Advanced Kitchen Eating

4.   Who is Mr. Swee Tuuth?

a doctor at J.O.K.E.

head of J.O.K.E.

the author of this article

5.   Who discovered the "junk" nutrient?

an anonymous junk food expert

Dr. Sill Ypants

Mr. Swee Tuuth

6.   Where did Mr. Tuuth first publish his observations?

in the newsletter of F.A.K.E.

in a report for J.O.K.E.

on online forums

7.   Why is the "junk" nutrient hard to uncover?

because of an abundance of toxins, fatty acids, and external chemicals

because it is hidden under layers of healthful nutrients

because of its complex nutritional make-up

B. Answer the questions.

> Satire in literature is used to critique the lack of judgment in people, society, or institutions through the use of humour.

1. What is the purpose of this satirical news article?

   _____

   _____

2. Who is the intended audience of this satire? Explain.

   _____

   _____

3.

   > *Do you think the use of acronyms is effective for this satire? Give examples from the article to support your answer.*

   _____

   _____

   _____

C. Write an example from the satirical news article for each feature below.

Features of Satire

- **Irony** (to convey the opposite of what is meant or intended)

  _____

  _____

- **Exaggeration** (to overstate something, often to expose faults)

  _____

  _____

- **Parody** (a mocking imitation of a person, a place, or a work's particular style)

  _____

  _____

D. **Read "Junk Food Is Good Food" again. Then look at the image below and answer the questions.**

 Illustrations in a satirical article help convey its intended message.

1. Write a caption for the image.

_____

2. Explain whether or not this image should replace the one in the satirical news article. Then write to complete the sentence.

_____

_____

Images of real people should not be used because _____

_____ .

My Notes

_____

_____

_____

_____

UNIT 4

Ms. Day's Class Survey

Ms. Day's Class Survey on Reading Habits

This survey was designed to assess the reading habits of Ms. Day's Grade 8 class. The results will help Ms. Day learn more about the class. Responses will be kept anonymous.

	Question	Always	Sometimes	Never	Total
1.	I enjoy reading in my spare time.	28	5	2	35
2.	I stop reading a book midway if I find it boring.	2	10	23	35
3.	I visualize the descriptions in the book to remember the details.	30	3	2	35
4.	When I do not understand something in a book, I change my reading strategy (e.g. re-read).	15	5	15	35
5.	I underline or highlight my favourite parts of the book.	14	6	15	35
6.	I make predictions as to what will happen next.	19	12	4	35
7.	I have reading goals that I try to achieve (e.g. read a chapter every day or read one book a month).	12	8	15	35
8.	I would rather do something else than read.	2	5	28	35
9.	I read everything I can find (e.g. cereal boxes, advertisements, etc.)	10	8	17	35

Question		Always	Sometimes	Never	Total
10.	I stick to one particular genre when picking what to read (e.g. mystery, historical fiction, romance, etc.)	7	18	10	35

In conclusion, it appears that most students in Ms. Day's class enjoy reading. A considerabe number of students practise good reading habits, though there is room for improvemnet. Ms. Day will use this information to help her cater to her class's needs.

A. Circle the answers.

1. What is the survey assessing?

   reading strategies

   reading habits

   reading purposes

2. Whom is the survey assessing?

   Ms. Day's Grade 8 students

   Ms. Day's Reading Club members

   Ms. Day's tutees

3. What does "responses will be kept anonymous" mean?

   Only Ms. Day can read the results.

   The students' names will not be shown.

   The students will not know the results.

4. How many students are there in Ms. Day's class?

   28

   30

   35

5. What do most students always do while reading?

   visualize the descriptions

   underline favourite parts

   make predictions

6. What does the survey conclude?

   No one enjoys reading.

   Everyone employs the same reading strategies.

   Most students in the class love reading.

B.   Answer the questions.

1.   What is the purpose of this survey?

_____

_____

> A survey is a research method used for compiling data from a set group of people.

2.   Is the format of the survey clear and easy to understand? Explain.

_____

_____

3.   Check the answers.

- This survey uses:

    Ⓐ   closed-ended questions (e.g. yes/no, multiple choice).

    Ⓑ   open-ended questions (e.g. essay, short answer).

- An alternative layout for the survey results could be:

    Ⓐ   a line graph.   Ⓑ   a pie chart.

- Ms. Day probably conducted the survey:

    Ⓐ   by asking each student questions in front of others.

    Ⓑ   by letting the students answer the survey questions on separate sheets of paper without their names on them.

C.   Read the questions. Rewrite them so that they are not biased.

🅐   Don't you agree that reading is a good habit?

🅑   There are many intelligent students who enjoy reading textbooks. Are you one of them?

> Unbiased questions are an important feature of a survey.
>
> Biased questions are not used because they encourage participants to respond in a certain way.

Unbiased

🅐   _____

🅑   _____

D. **Read "Ms. Day's Class Survey" again and fill in the information.**

Survey
☑ ——
☑ ——
☑ ——
☑ ——
☑ ☑——

Three facts I have learned about the reading habits of Ms. Day's class from the survey:

e.g. Most students in Ms. Day's class enjoy reading in their spare time.

Facts:

1. _____

   _____

2. _____

   _____

3. _____

   _____

Questions
——
——
——

Three additional questions I think should be included in Ms. Day's class survey:

Remember to ask unbiased questions.

Questions:

1. _____

   _____

2. _____

   _____

3. _____

   _____

My Notes

_____

_____

_____

_____

UNIT

5 **Canadian English Thesaurus**

---

blamable   p. 102   **bleary**

400. **blamable** *adj.* answerable, blameworthy, culpable, faulty, guilty, liable, responsible

401. **blameless** *adj.* clean, clear, faultless, guiltless, immaculate

402. **bland** *adj.* (1) boring, dull, flat, monotonous, tasteless, tedious (2) amiable, courteous, gentle

403. **blank** *adj.* (1) bare, clean, clear, empty, plain, spotless (2) dull, empty, expressionless

404. **blanket** *n.* (1) cover, rug (2) carpet, cloak, coat, envelope *adj.* (3) comprehensive, overall

405. **blare** *v.* blast, boom, clamour, clang, honk, hoot, roar, scream, toot, trumpet

406. **blast** *n./v.* (1) blare, blow, clang, 1700; scream *n.* (2) burst, crash, 702; explosion, outburst (3) gale, storm, tempest *v.* (4) attack, criticize, put down

407. **blatant** *adj.* (1) bold, brazen, flaunting, glaring (2) clamorous, deafening, harsh, loud, noisy

408. **blaze** *n.* (1) bonfire, conflagration, fire, flame *v.* (2) beam, flare, glare, glow

409. **bleary** *adj.* blurred, dim, foggy, fuzzy, hazy, indistinct, misty, murky, watery

CANADIAN ENGLISH THESAURUS

A.   Circle the answers.

1.   What is the thesaurus called?

Canadian English Thesaurus

Canadian Thesaurus

Canadian English Dictionary

2.   What is the thesaurus used for?

finding the origins of words

finding the homophones of words

finding the synonyms of words

3.   Which letter do all the word entries begin with?

A

B

C

4.   What does this stand for?

noun

adverb

adjective

adj.

p. 975

INDEX

Word entries are numbered and placed in alphabetical order within a thesaurus. The numbers in the index refer to the word entry numbers next to which the word entries are placed.

When a word is used under another word entry, it is set in italics in the index and numbered according to the place in which it appears as its own entry in the thesaurus. This way, the word appears only once in the index, placed according to its meaning, to help save space and make its location clear to the user.

B

Babble	339	Badly	358	Blamable	400	Blast	406
Baby	345	*carelessly*	466	Blameless	401	*scream*	1700
Back	356	*evily*	699	Bland	402	*explosion*	702
Backbone	357	Balanced	369	Blank	403	Blatant	407
spinal column	1929	Balloon	370	Blanket	404	Blaze	408
foundation	991	Beaming	381	Blare	405	Bleary	409

CANADIAN ENGLISH THESAURUS

5. What does "scream 1700" placed under the word entry "Blast" in the index mean?

The word "scream" has its own word entry number.

This is the number of times that "scream" appears in the thesaurus.

This is the number of synonyms that "scream" has.

6. How many different ways can this word be used according to the thesaurus?

blanket

nine

six

three

B. **Write the purposes for the features of the "Canadian English Thesaurus".**

A thesaurus is a book that alphabetically lists words in groups of synonyms or related concepts.

Traditionally, an alphabetical index with numbered word entries is used to locate a word.

Feature **Purpose**

CANADIAN ENGLISH THESAURUS

A Index: _____

B Guide Word: _____

C Word Entry Number: _____

D Number in Parentheses: _____

E Word in Bold: _____

F Word in Italics in the Index: _____

C. **Fill in the blanks with words from the "Canadian English Thesaurus". The synonyms of the words are given in parentheses.**

1. I am not _____ (answerable) for the damage.

2. The food that I made tasted _____ (tasteless).

3. I need a _____ (blanket) because I feel very cold.

4. There was an _____ (blast) in the science laboratory.

5. The police will _____ (blow) the door open.

6. Anna stared at her sister as she told her a _____ (brazen) lie.

7. The _____ (blanket) statement covered all aspects of the problem.

8. Julius could barely see through his _____ (watery) eyes.

D. Check to show whether or not you would use the "Canadian English Thesaurus" in the following situations. Then use a thesaurus of your own to write the synonyms of the given word entries.

I would use this thesaurus to find:

> It would be helpful to use a thesaurus to find synonyms.
> Use the alphabetical order in the index and the word entry number in the thesaurus to locate a word.

Ⓐ the antonym of a word

Ⓑ the homophone of a word

Ⓒ the synonym of a word

Ⓓ the definition of a word

Ⓔ the related concepts of a word

Ⓕ a better replacement of a word

THESAURUS

haste

harness _____
_____
_____

harvest _____
_____
_____

harsh _____
_____
_____

haste _____
_____
_____

My Notes

_____
_____
_____
_____

UNIT

6 Water Pollution

Problem

Water pollution is negatively affecting our environment.

Definition

🍃 contamination of water bodies (e.g. lakes, rivers, oceans), usually as a result of human activity

🍃 occurs when pollutants are directly or indirectly discharged into water bodies without adequate treatment to remove harmful substances such as toxic chemicals from factories

🍃 Types of Water Pollution:

- groundwater pollution
- surface water pollution
- ocean water pollution
- nutrient pollution
- suspended matter pollution
- microbiological water pollution
- chemical water pollution
- sewage pollution
- oxygen depletion
- oil spillage

Causes

🍃 discharge of waste directly into water bodies due to the lack of waste management systems

🍃 seepage of sewage, fertilizers, and pesticides through groundwater into other water bodies

🍃 leakage of pollutants from landfills into water bodies

🍃 disposal of trash and toxic or chemical materials into water bodies

🍃 oil spills

🍃 burning of fossil fuels leading to air pollution, consequently contaminating rainwater

Effects

🍃 death of aquatic animals

🍃 disruption of food chains and destruction of ecosystems

🍃 lack of clean, consumable water

🍃 susceptibility to certain diseases through drinking contaminated water and eating diseased aquatic animals

🍃 flooding due to the accumulation of solid waste and soil erosion in water bodies

A. Circle the answers.

1. What is water pollution?

   the disposal of chemicals

   the disruption of food chains

   the contamination of water bodies

2. How is water polluted?

   when we reduce, reuse, and recycle

   when trees are planted

   when pollutants are discharged into water bodies

3. Which is not a type of water pollution?

   soil erosion

   oxygen depletion

   oil spillage

4. What is a cause of water pollution?

   death of aquatic animals

   burning of fossil fuels

   using eco-friendly products

5. What is an effect of water pollution?

   contaminated drinking water

   contaminated rainwater

   oil spills

6. Which is not a solution to water pollution?

   using water wisely

   supporting anti-pollution policies

   using fertilizers and pesticides

Solutions

- reduce, reuse, recycle
- dispose of chemicals, oils, paints, and medicine responsibly
- use eco-friendly products but keep that at a minimum too
- plant trees to clean the environment
- use water wisely and sparingly
- support anti-pollution laws and policies
- educate others on the effects and solutions of water pollution

B. Check the true statements and put a cross for the false ones.

1. Water pollution is usually the result of natural occurrences. ◯

2. Oxygen depletion, chemical matter, and oil spillage are types of water pollution. ◯

3. The burning of fossil fuels pollutes water through rainfall. ◯

4. Aquatic animals can live in highly polluted water bodies. ◯

5. Humans can catch diseases from drinking contaminated water. ◯

6. Water pollution only occurs when pollutants are directly discharged into water bodies. ◯

7. Disposing of chemicals, oils, paints, and medicine responsibly is a solution to water pollution. ◯

C. Answer the questions.

1. Define water pollution in your own words.

_____

_____

2. Describe the cause and effect relationship of water pollution using one example from the text.

_____

_____

_____

3. Suggest an additional solution to help reduce water pollution.

_____

_____

D. Complete the problem and solution map by writing the letters of the additional information about water pollution in the correct categories.

Problem and Solution Map

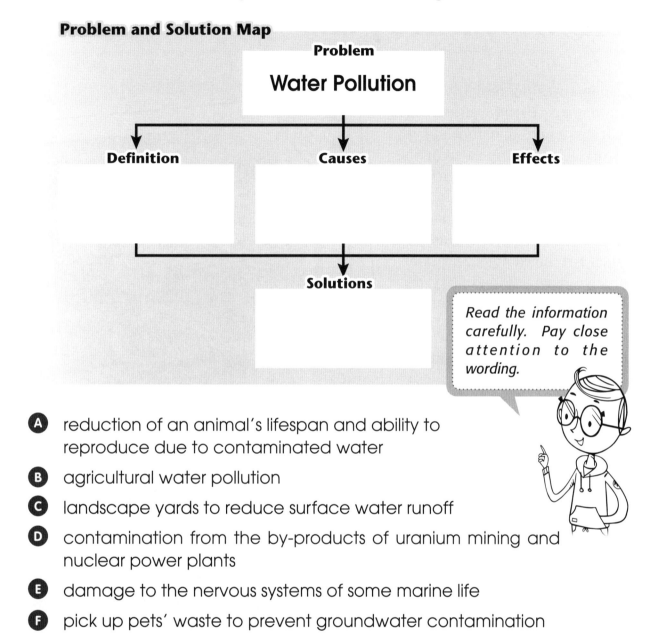

A reduction of an animal's lifespan and ability to reproduce due to contaminated water

B agricultural water pollution

C landscape yards to reduce surface water runoff

D contamination from the by-products of uranium mining and nuclear power plants

E damage to the nervous systems of some marine life

F pick up pets' waste to prevent groundwater contamination

My Notes

_____

_____

_____

_____

UNIT 7 Just Like Grandma Used to Make – A Memoir by Mia

My grandma was my best friend as I was growing up. Usually, when I came home from school and finished my homework, I would help her in the kitchen. I loved cooking with my grandma. She was the best chef, even better than my mom, but I would never tell my mom that. On special occasions, like when I received a good mark at school, my grandma would make my favourite dessert – cherry pie.

No other cherry pie could beat my grandma's. Not only did she make everything from scratch but she also made it with love and care. Whenever we baked her famous pie, we would play smooth jazz music in the background. The neighbours downstairs probably hated the clickety-clack of our shoes tapping on the hard kitchen floor as we danced to the music and twirled in our matching aprons.

Grandma & Me

To make my grandma's famous cherry pie, we started with the crust. We mixed all the ingredients together and then my grandma would roll and shape the dough with her soft but firm hands. After placing the dough in the pan, we poured in the cherry filling. I could not help but steal a couple of cherries as my grandma swatted my little hands away.

Then I would wait impatiently in front of the oven, straining to hear the ding of the timer. As soon as it was finished baking, my grandma would nudge me to the side as she carefully took out the pie. I was always too impatient to wait for it to cool so my grandma would warn me, "Mia, dearie, you'll burn the roof of your mouth!"

Finally, when the pie was cool enough to eat, my grandma and I would share a big slice and top it off with a cold scoop of vanilla ice cream. The warm, tart cherry mixed with the cool, sweet vanilla made for the perfect treat after school or on weekends. Some days, my grandma would even let me have it for breakfast!

My grandma passed away when I was in elementary school, but her lessons and memory still live on. She was the one who inspired me to become a chef. She made all her dishes with love and care, and that is what I want to do too. Like her, I want to share love in the form of food with the world. Of course, I will never be as good as my grandma, but I hope to make her proud and keep her memory alive.

A.　Circle the answers.

1. Whom is the memoir about?

   Mia and baking

   Mia's mom and Mia's grandma

   Mia and her grandma

2. Who wrote the memoir?

   Mia

   Mia and her mom

   Mia and her grandma

3. What is Mia's favourite dessert?

   cherry tart

   cherry pie

   vanilla ice cream

4. When did Mia's grandma make Mia's favourite dessert?

   when Mia came home from school every day

   on special occasions

   every weekend

5. What did their neighbours downstairs probably hate?

   the sound of the jazz music

   the smell of the cherry pie

   the tapping of their shoes as they danced

6. What did Mia's grandma call her?

   cherry pie

   dearie

   beanie

7. What did Mia and her grandma eat with the pie?

   vanilla ice cream

   vanilla beans

   cherry ice cream

8. What did Mia's grandma make all her dishes with?

   cherries and ice cream

   both warm and cool ingredients

   love and care

B.   Answer the questions.

1.   What is the significance of Mia's relationship with her grandmother?

_____

_____,

_____

> A memoir focuses on the relationship between the writer and a particular person, place, animal, or object. It is limited to a particular time period and setting, and uses the first person point of view.

2.   Write the step-by-step instructions for making cherry pie the way Mia's grandmother used to make it.

Instructions for Grandma's Cherry Pie

Steps

1.   _____

2.   _____

3.   _____

4.   _____

5.   _____

C.   Write sentences from the text to support the statements.

1.   Mia is a chef.

_____

2.   Mia and her grandmother liked music.

_____

3.   Mia's grandmother did not bake cherry pies too often.

_____

4.   Mia cares about her mom's feelings.

_____

5.   Mia misses her grandmother.

_____

D. Read the text. Then answer the question.

"...could not help but steal a couple of cherries as my grandma swatted my little hands away.

Then I would wait impatiently in front of the oven, straining to hear the ding of the timer. As soon as it was finished baking, my grandma would nudge me to the side as she carefully took out the pie. I was always too impatient to wait for it to cool so my grandma would warn me, "Mia, dearie, you'll burn the roof of your mouth!"

What does the text show about how Mia's grandmother felt about Mia and making cherry pies with her?

_____

_____

_____

_____

_____

_____

_____

_____

_____

My Notes

_____

_____

_____

_____

UNIT

8

Springville High School Student Transcript

 SPRINGVILLE HIGH SCHOOL

STUDENT ACADEMIC RECORD

Name: **Smith, John**   Address: 123 Springville Ave., Springville, AB. xxx-xxx

D.O.B.: **MAY 27, 2001**   Student Number: N12345   Graduation Date: JUNE 30, 2019

School Year: 2015 – 2016   Grade Level: 9

Course	Credit Earned	Percentage Grade
English	1	75
Math	1	78
Science	1	77
Physical Education	1	85
History	1	76
Art and Music	1	85
French	1	77
Computer Science	1	85
		80

School Year: 2016 – 2017   Grade Level: 10

Course	Credit Earned	Percentage Grade
English	1	77
Math	1	79
Science	1	78
Canadian and World Studies	1	77
Computer Science	1	87
Introduction to Business	1	79
Music	1	85
French	1	79
		80

School Year: 2017 – 2018   Grade Level: 11

Course	Credit Earned	Percentage Grade
English	1	85
Math	1	85
Computer Science	1	83
French	1	83
Business	1	85
Music	1	88
World History	1	80
Independent Study	1	N/A
		84

School Year: 2018 – 2019   Grade Level: 12

Course	Credit Earned	Percentage Grade
English	1	88
Calculus	1	88
Data Management	1	90
Accounting	1	85
French	1	87
Business	1	88
		88

Academic Summary

Cumulative G.P.A.:	83
Credits Earned:	30
Community Hours Earned:	40
Diploma Earned:	Yes

I do hereby certify that this is the official transcript of John Smith.

M. Patson
_____
Miles Patson, Principal

June 30, 2019
Date

This is the school transcript of student John Smith. A transcript is an official record of a student's academic history, showing the courses the student took and the grades that he or she achieved at each grade level.

A. Circle the answers.

1. The academic record of how many years is shown on the transcript?

   two

   four

   six

2. What does "D.O.B." stand for?

   Deposit of Budget

   Date of Business

   Date of Birth

3. How many credits did the student earn?

   30

   40

   83

4. How old was the student in Grade 10?

   10 years old

   12 years old

   16 years old

5. In which course did the student not achieve a percentage grade?

   Independent Study

   History

   Physical Education

6. Which courses did the student take every year?

   English and Science

   French and English

   English and Computer Science

7. In which school year did the student take the fewest courses?

   2016 – 2017

   2017 – 2018

   2018 – 2019

8. At which grade level did the student achieve the highest overall grade?

   10

   11

   12

B. **Read the descriptions and write the correct features on the lines.**

> credit   student number   percentage grade   cumulative G.P.A.
>
> community hours   grade level   principal's signature

1. _____ : an individual number given to each student to help identify him or her

2. _____ : the overall grade point average

3. _____ : the time spent volunteering in order to graduate

4. _____ : the educational stage a student is at

5. _____ : a unit used to determine the completion and passing of a course

6. _____ : used to certify a true and correct account of a student's achievements

7. _____ : a unit used to assess a student's work and mastery of a subject

C. **Answer the questions.**

1. What purpose would John Smith's transcript serve for the following people?

 A student's transcript can help him or her make informed choices about his or her education. It can also be used by other personnel to assess the student's academic performance.

 John Smith

_____

 John Smith's Basketball Coach

_____

 Springville High School's Student Counsellor

_____

2. Which features of this transcript would help set it apart from a transcript issued by another school?

_____

_____

D. Read John Smith's Springville High School transcript again and answer the questions.

1. Compare John's academic performances in Grade 9 and Grade 10 and explain his progress. Give examples.

Remember to consider improvements in grades, changes in courses, highest grades achieved, and more.

_____

_____

_____

_____

_____

2.

I am not sure whether to pursue English, Math, or French after high school.

Write to compare John's grades in the subjects from each grade level to help him decide.

Subject	Grade 9	Grade 10	Grade 11	Grade 12
English				
Math				
French				

John Smith should pursue _____ after high school because

_____

_____

My Notes

_____

_____

_____

_____

UNIT 9 Beppu, Japan

World Travel Magazine

Login   Create Account   Print   Subscribe   Search

| Home | Travel Tips | City Guides | Articles | News |

The Hottest City in Japan - Beppu

October 2018
Text: Jessie L.

Traditional Japanese culture is renowned for its peaceful aesthetic. There is no better way to experience it than to head to one of Japan's most delightful attractions – the outdoor hot spring bath. In particular, we head to Beppu, Japan – a beautiful, coastal city best known for its hot springs.

Beppu is located on the west end of Beppu Bay in the Oita Prefecture on the southern main island of Kyushu. It is flanked along the back by Mt. Tsurumi and a ridge of hills. Because Japan is located atop shifting tectonic plates, it is a site of frequent earthquakes and geothermal activity, forming hot springs that can be found from one end of the country to the other. Here in Beppu, these thermal dynamics are displayed most spectacularly and serenely in the beautiful countryside.

Beppu has a population of over 122 000. This resort city is considered the *onsen* (meaning "hot spring" in Japanese) capital of Japan. There are also *rotenburos*

The beautiful city of Beppu, Japan

(outdoor hot spring baths) that can range from human-made pools outside hotel rooms to the most splendid natural pools surrounded by dense vegetation. These hot springs are not only relaxing, but are claimed to have healing properties as well, with cures for everything from diabetes to psoriasis to arthritis.

Beppu is also known for its nine *jigoku* or "hells", which are hot springs (primarily tourist sites, not baths) of various sizes, colours, and mineral content, as well as bubbling mud pots and geysers surrounded by botanical gardens. The *umi-jigoku* (sea hell) is a bright cobalt blue, while the *chi-no-ike jigoku* (blood pond hell) holds deep rust-coloured water. At Takegawara Spa, one can take a *suna-yu*, or sand bath,

"These hot springs are not only relaxing, but are claimed to have healing properties as well..."

as well as a mud bath.

Soaking in an outdoor hot spring bath after a hike in the mountains, with *yuzu* (a large locally-grown citrus fruit) bobbing around in the water, followed by a hearty Japanese meal in front of an open hearth at a traditional inn, would be an unforgettable delight.

If you are intrigued by geothermal energy and want to relax on your vacation, then you will certainly want to pay a visit to Japan and the "steaming" resort city of Beppu.

Other Attractions in Beppu:

- Beppu Park

- Mount Tsurumi

- Takasakiyama Monkey Park

19/64

A.   Circle the answers.

1.   What is the name of the online magazine?

City Guides

World Travel Magazine

Jessie L.

2.   What is Beppu, Japan best known for?

its *onsen*

its *yuzu*

its *suna-yu*

3.   Where is the Oita Prefecture?

on the west end of Beppu Bay

in Kyushu

on Mt. Tsurumi

4.   What are hot springs claimed to have?

a peaceful aesthetic

dense vegetation

healing properties

5.   What colour is the famous *chi-no-ike jigoku*?

bright blue

orange red

light yellow

6.   Where can a tourist take a sand bath or a mud bath?

at Beppu Park

on Mt. Tsurumi

at Takegawara Spa

B. Answer the questions.

1. What is the purpose of this online magazine article?

   _____

2. Who might be the intended audience? Explain.

   _____

3. Why are there so many hot springs in Japan?

   _____

   _____

4. Do you think an effective pull-quote is used for the article?

   _____

   _____

 A pull-quote is an excerpt that is pulled from the text and used as an attention-catching graphic element.

C. Write "F" for facts and "O" for opinions.

 Magazine articles use facts to support the expressed opinion.

A fact is a statement that can be proven true or false. An opinion is a personal belief or feeling.

Fact/Opinion

1. In particular, we head to Beppu, Japan, a beautiful, coastal city best known for its hot springs.   _____

2. Beppu is located on the west end of Beppu Bay.   _____

3. Japan is located atop shifting tectonic plates.   _____

4. These thermal dynamics are displayed most spectacularly and serenely in this beautiful countryside.   _____

5. Beppu has a population of over 122 000.   _____

6. These hot springs are not only relaxing, but are claimed to have healing properties as well.   _____

D. **Read the online magazine article again and check to identify its features. Then write to suggest changes in text and features to increase the number of subscribers.**

 An online magazine relies on its subscribers to maintain its success.

Features of an Online Magazine

Ⓐ visual storytelling   Ⓑ linear navigation   Ⓒ caption

Ⓓ feature article   Ⓔ subheadings   Ⓕ logo

Ⓖ subscribe button   Ⓗ search box   Ⓘ "About Me" section

Changes in Text

_____

_____

_____

_____

_____

Changes in Features

_____

_____

_____

_____

_____

My Notes

_____

_____

_____

_____

UNIT

10 Stress Management

Memo

To: All Employees
From: Martin Wright
Date: December 2, 2019
Subject: Stress Management

The holidays and our end-of-year deadlines are fast approaching, and we know how stressful work can be at this hectic time of year. Here are some tips for all employees on how to manage stress.

Studies have shown that stress has an adverse effect on our bodies; our blood pressure, body temperature, and heart rate rise due to stress. After long-term stress exposure, our reaction times decrease, our mental functions start to slip, and we may suffer from insomnia, depression, or anger outbursts.

Keeping this in mind, we want to encourage all of our employees to practise de-stressing techniques and self-care both at work and at home. We suggest trying meditation and relaxation; both are good ways to help reduce the effects of stress. Our other suggestions include:

- going for a 10-minute walk every day
- exercising regularly and maintaining a healthful diet
- taking short breaks
- speaking with someone about how you feel
- making time for hobbies

If you find something else that helps you de-stress, we encourage you to try it and share it with others.

We will also be hosting a "de-stress hour" for those who would like to participate. It will be held on December 6, 2019 at 2 p.m. in the main conference room. Refreshments will be provided.

We will also e-mail you articles on stress management if you would like more information.

Here at Smart Company, we care about each of our employees, knowing that our office will be at its most productive if you are happy and satisfied with the work environment. If you require any assistance, please feel free to reach out to the Human Resources Department located on the third floor of the main building.

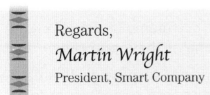

Regards,

Martin Wright

President, Smart Company

A. Circle the answers.

1. For whom is the office memo?

   all the employers at Smart Company

   all the employees at Smart Company

   the president of Smart Company

2. What does "adverse" in Paragraph 2 mean?

   harmful

   healthful

   positive

3. What effect does stress have on our bodies?

   a decrease in blood pressure

   fluctuating body temperature

   a rise in heart rate

4. What effect does long-term stress have on our bodies?

   insomnia

   improved mental functions

   increased reaction times

5. When will the de-stress session be held?

   in the morning of December 6

   during lunchtime on December 6

   in the afternoon of December 6

6. Where will the de-stress session be held?

   in the main conference room

   in the Human Resources Department

   on the third floor of the main building

7. What information will be e-mailed to individual employees upon request?

   articles on meditation

   articles on stress management

   the refreshment list

8. Who is Martin Wright?

   the president

   the president's secretary

   the head of the Human Resources Department

B.   Answer the questions.

1.   What is the purpose of this memo?

_____

_____

> An office memo (memorandum) has one of these purposes:
>
> to inform, to provide feedback or a response, to address or solve an issue, or to make a request.

2.   Why are short paragraphs and bullet points used in the memo?

_____

_____

3.   Is the memo written objectively or subjectively?

_____

4.   In your opinion, why is the de-stress session optional for the employees?

_____

_____

5.   Who or what is Martin Wright representing? Why?

_____

_____

6.   What content is covered in the following parts of the memo?

Header: _____

_____

_____

> A memo has a header and a message.
>
> The message consists of an introduction, a body, and a conclusion.

Introduction: _____

Body: _____

_____

_____

Conclusion: _____

_____

C. Read "Stress Management" again. Then fill in the information in your own words and write about how you de-stress. Draw your face in the circle.

Causes of stress:

_____

_____

_____

_____

Effects of stress:

_____

_____

_____

_____

De-stressing techniques:

_____

_____

_____

_____

Steps taken by Smart Company to help its employees manage stress:

_____

_____

_____

_____

Reasons why Smart Company wants its employees to de-stress:

_____

_____

_____

_____

Techniques I use to de-stress:

_____

_____

_____

My Notes

_____

_____

_____

_____

WeConnect

www.weconnect.pop.ca

WeConnect

Sign Out | Profile | About

My Page
News Feed
Events
Friends
Photos
Saved Items

Chat

Groups
Book Club 2
Science Project
School Committee
Math Tutor
▼ more

Friends
Michael M.
▼ more

Advertisement

New
$19.99

News Feed

Craft Club Post   Today

Remember to come to our meeting on May 5!

Like   Comment   Share

Michael M. Post   Yesterday

Hello everyone,
I need help with my Math homework. Can anyone help me?

Like   Comment   Share

Mr. Perez's Science Class Post   Monday

Hello everyone,
Remember that we have a test on May 8! Do not be late!

Like   Comment   Share

Stacy M. Shared Post   Last Week

Sign this petition to encourage school uniforms! <u>Click here!</u>

Like   Comment   Share

Top News

1. *Pop City High School Wins Gold in Soccer*
2. *Math Team Moves onto Regional Tournament*
3. *Principal Lahiri is Retiring*

Events

- **May 5**
  Craft Club meeting at 3:30 p.m.
- **May 6**
  Book Club meeting at 3:30 p.m.

Saved Items

- *Video "How to Knit"*
- *Article "Why I Chose to go to University"*
- *Website "The Daily News"*

> *This is a social networking website called "WeConnect". A social networking site is a website through which users interact with others and share information. People use these websites to connect with others who share similar interests or connections, and to build a social network.*

A. Circle the answers.

1. Which posts appear at the top of the news feed?

   the most recent

   the oldest

   at random

2. What can a user do to a news feed post?

   Link, post, and follow it.

   Comment, share, and like it.

   Click, save, and post it.

3. How is the chat section organized?

   in alphabetical order

   by group and friend

   by date

4. What is the advertisement selling?

   a telescope

   a microscope

   a kaleidoscope

5. What type of news appears in the news section?

   national

   community

   local school

6. Who is retiring?

   Michael M.

   Mr. Perez

   the principal

7. How is the event section organized?

   by group

   by importance

   by date

8. When will the Book Club meet?

   on May 5 at 3:30 p.m.

   on May 6 at 2:30 p.m.

   on May 6 at 3:30 p.m.

B. **Match the features of a social networking website with their descriptions. Write the letters.**

A news feed   _____   a graphic element that holds information and is placed alongside the main content

B profile   _____   used to mark content to be viewed later

C home page   _____   a list of new updates, posts, and information

     _____   a personal account with the user's information

D sidebar

     _____   used to alert the user to the number of unread messages he or she has received

E saved item

     _____   the main webpage that shows all the features of the site when the site is first opened

F search bar

G notification   _____   a graphic element that allows the user to look something up

C. **Answer the questions.**

1. What is the purpose of the social networking website "WeConnect"?

    _____

    _____

2. Who would use this website?

    _____

    _____

3. Do you think the layout of "WeConnect" is user-friendly? Why or why not?

    _____

> A user-friendly website is designed to be accessible, simple, and easy to navigate.

    _____

    _____

D. **Look at the social networking website "WeConnect" again and answer the questions.**

1. Write two features you would include to make the website more user-friendly. Explain their purposes.

Feature

Purpose: _____

_____

_____

_____

_____

Feature

Purpose: _____

_____

_____

_____

_____

2. Write three advantages and three disadvantages of using similar social networking sites.

Advantage	_____ _____ _____
Disadvantage	_____ _____ _____

My Notes

_____

_____

_____

_____

A. Circle the answers.

1. The elements of a plot diagram for a short story are in this order:

   exposition, falling action, rising action, climax, resolution

   exposition, rising action, climax, falling action, resolution

   exposition, climax, rising action, falling action, resolution

2. A prologue is addressed to the audience _____ of a play.

   at the opening

   in the middle

   at the end

3. What is a soliloquy?

   a character's opponent

   a character's speech to himself or herself

   the props that a character uses

4. Satire in literature is used to criticize the lack of judgment through the use of _____ .

   humour

   facts and figures

   pictures of real people

5. What is the purpose of a survey?

   to entertain

   to inform

   to advertise

6. Which type of questions are asked in a survey?

   unbiased questions

   biased questions

   open-ended questions

7. A thesaurus is a book used to find the _____ of words.

   definitions

   synonyms

   rhyming words

8. Which is not a feature of a thesaurus?

   guide word

   index

   legend

9. What are the subheadings in a problem and solution map?

   problem, definition, causes, effects, solutions

   problem, title, causes, solutions

   problem, solution

10. A problem and solution map uses _____ .

   maps

   arrows

   long paragraphs

11. Which text type focuses on the relationship between the writer and a particular person, place, animal, or object?

12. A memoir uses the _____ .

    first person point of view

    second person point of view

    third person point of view

13. The _____ certifies that a transcript is a true and correct account of a student's academic achievements.

    grade level

    cumulative G.P.A.

    principal's signature

14. Who would use a student's transcript?

    the student's doctor

    the student's school counsellor

    the student's best friend

15. What is a pull-quote used as?

    an advertising scheme

    an attention-catching graphic element

    a literary device in an online magazine

16. Which statement defines a fact?

    A fact can be proven true or false.

    A fact cannot be proven true or false.

    A fact is a personal expression of feelings.

17. What does an online magazine rely on for success?

    its subscribers

    the number of "pages" it has

    its pull-quotes

18. Which is not a purpose of an office memo?

    to inform

    to provide feedback

    to entertain

19. A social networking website has the _____ as the main webpage.

    sidebar

    home page

    news feed

20. Where would you type to look up information on a social networking website?

    in the sidebar

    in the saved items

    in the search bar

B.   Read the short story and check to show whether the statements are true or false.

Rider's Dilemma

Rider was a young man who worked as a writer for a small publishing firm called Write Away. For as long as he could easily remember, he could write all types of stories, articles, reports, poems, and much more. However, lately, there had been days when he was unable to cope with the amount of work he was charged with and did not know whether he should tackle everything simultaneously or write one piece of text at a time.

On one such day, he was having a particularly hard time because Penn, his manager, had tasked him with writing a poem about a firefly that had lost its way, a report on Canada's immigration patterns, and a fairy tale about a stubborn elf. These writing assignments were drastically different from one another, yet they were all equally important, so he did not know which to complete first. As the assignments piled up and their deadlines loomed like unconquerable towers on his desk, Rider panicked and took on all the text types at the same time, thinking it was better to just get them all out of the way at once.

He wrote down pairs of rhyming words for the poem until he hit the writer's block. "More like Rider's block," he muttered to himself. He then decided to trudge through and start the next assignment. He looked up the statistical data for the report, shoving his poetry notes aside and piling new sheets on top. But Rider quickly became overwhelmed with the magnitude of information online, so he paused and began writing the outline for the fairy tale instead. At this point, even the fairy tale seemed like a menacing monster. Looking down at the mess of scattered sheets of paper on his desk, Rider sighed in frustration. He would never get anything done like this!

After taking a moment to sit back and reflect on his predicament, Rider decided to use an alternative strategy and work only on one task at a time. He organized his sheets of paper into neat, coordinated piles and cleared his desk of clutter. He then took a few minutes to calm down and brainstorm ideas for the poem, which he decided he would focus on first. When he believed he had good ideas for his poem, he dived into his work and created a clear outline of what he would write. As a result of this new strategy and his careful planning, Rider was able to complete all his work before the deadlines.

1. Rider works as the manager at Write Away. ☐ ☐

2. Rider can use one of two strategies to meet the deadlines. ☐ ☐

3. Rider has to write three different text types. ☐ ☐

4. Rider has to write about a stubborn firefly and a lost elf. ☐ ☐

5. Rider clears his desk of clutter before brainstorming ideas for his poem. ☐ ☐

6. Doing all the assignments at the same time is the most effective strategy for Rider. ☐ ☐

7. Penn is the protagonist of the story. ☐ ☐

C. Answer the questions.

1. What is the moral of the short story?

    _____

    _____

2. Circle to identify the type of conflict Rider faces. Then write to explain your answer.

    physical   environmental   social   psychological

    _____

    _____

3. What is the resolution of the short story?

    _____

    _____

4. Suggest another strategy to help Rider manage the deadlines.

    _____

    _____

D. **Read the satirical report. Then answer the questions.**

Procrastination Is the Key to Success!

By Penn Parker

An ongoing study being conducted by the I.D.L.E. (Internal Delegation of Lazy Employees) at Write Away is getting closer and closer to proving that procrastination, and not hard work, is the key to success after all! The study, which began a decade ago and is not yet complete, focuses on the working habits of a select few employees at Write Away. So far, I.D.L.E. researchers have observed that the common habits of procrastinators include: scrolling through social media during work hours, daydreaming at their desks, and avoiding doing work in hopes that it will finish itself.

When asked how these habits have been proving beneficial to success at work, Mr. Tyrdan Sluggesh, a member of I.D.L.E., said, "Well, my fellow I.D.L.E. researchers and I have noticed that when employees do not focus on work and avoid doing it, they have to work twice as hard and fast at the last minute to finish it. Sure, they may not produce great quality work because of this, but the adrenaline from all the stress they experience when trying to frantically meet deadlines means that thoughts of work keep them up at night. And isn't that what every working person wants – to be thinking about work every waking hour of the day?"

1. What is the purpose of this satire?

   _____

   _____

2. Who is the intended audience of this satire?

   _____

3. Give an example from the text for each feature of this satire.

   Irony: _____

   _____

   Exaggeration: _____

   _____

E. Read the memo and write the letters in the circles to label the features of the memo. Then answer the questions.

(1) → **Write Away**

Memo

To: All Staff   ← (2)
From: Penn Parker, Manager
Date: November 20, 2019
Subject: Improper Use of Company Time

(3)

Features of a Memo

A	company's name	**B**	conclusion
C	header	**D**	recipient
E	introduction	**F**	body

It has come to the management's attention that a few employees have been spending working hours on holiday planning. This memo is a reminder to utilize your work hours productively.

(4)

Some of the unproductive activities noticed by the management are:
· using office computers to schedule personal days
· coordinating and organizing family calendars during work hours
· buying gifts online for the holidays

(5)

According to our estimates, Write Away is incurring a daily loss of $1500 based on the decreased productivity at work due to the time taken for holiday planning.

Therefore, we urge all employees to be more considerate with the use of company time while still maintaining a rewarding environment. Thank you.

(6)

Penn Parker
Manager, Write Away

7. What is the main purpose of this memo?

_____

_____

8. Why are bullet points used in this memo?

_____

9. Is this memo written objectively or subjectively? Explain.

_____

_____

Section 4

Writing

UNIT 1

Developing Ideas

Music – The Most Reliable Therapy

For people who want to relax, de-stress, or heal their minds and bodies, music has been one of the most reliable therapies since the beginning of time. Cave dwellers fashioned musical instruments from animal bone, ancient Egyptians made it an integral part of funeral rituals – even Aristotle and Plato wrote about it. For most people today, music is an integral part of everyday life. They listen to music on their commute, while exercising, or while doing other mundane tasks, like cooking or doing laundry. People turn to music as a way to relax, refresh, and rejuvenate their minds, or as an escape from their daily struggles.

Music has also been proven to have certain health benefits. Research has shown that when a person listens to music, his or her brain releases dopamine, a neurotransmitter that makes him or her feel good and happy. Music also decreases blood pressure and the amount of the stress hormone cortisol in the body and thus counteracts the effects of chronic stress. Furthermore, research has also proven that listening to music can help people sleep better, manage pain, and strengthen their learning ability and memory. With all of these amazing benefits, it is no wonder that most people turn to music.

In recent years, music and its therapeutic qualities have become an important element in nursing homes, hospitals, and rehabilitation centres. It was popularized after World War II as a community service when musicians were invited to perform for soldiers in hospitals to help them overcome the mental and physical traumas of combat. Since then, music as a form of therapy has expanded in all directions; it is now called upon to work its magic on newborns – even pre-borns. It has made the jump from humans to animals and plants as well; the idea of calming your pet or helping your plants grow faster with a bit of Mozart is no longer something to snicker at.

There are, however, some important things people should consider when choosing music to help them de-stress. Ideally, the music should be relaxing and not too loud. Even soothing music at an incorrect volume will prevent relaxation. Also, there is some risk involved in using pop music. Even if a pop song has a calming tone and beat, it could have mental connections to experiences in the listener's life that could make relaxation difficult. The words in songs can act as a trigger to bad memories. For this reason, music with lyrics should be avoided.

No matter where and when music is incorporated into a person's life, he or she can benefit from it in many ways. It is no wonder that music remains an effective alternative to traditional forms of therapy.

A. Read the text and fill in the information or check the answers.

1. Intended Audience:

   _____

   _____

2. Purposes:

   ◯ to explain   ◯ to inform

   ◯ to instruct   ◯ to critique

   ◯ to persuade   ◯ to entertain

> Writers need to define the audience and purpose of their writing because it will affect its form and content. Good writers anticipate the readers' needs and consider the questions they may have to help develop ideas, choose the best form, and provide a direction for research.

3. Topic: _____

4. Three Important Facts from the Text:

   • _____

   • _____

   • _____

5. One Question You Have about the Topic:

   _____

Clustering is a form of pre-writing that involves jotting down any words or phrases related to an idea that come to mind without pondering over the text itself. At this stage, do not focus too much on organization as this may impede the free flow of ideas. Do not cross anything out either as those ideas may be useful later.

B. **In no more than ten minutes, write down as many ideas as you can on "Pet Therapy". Then consider the questions that readers may have about the topic.**

Pet Therapy

 Ideas

 Readers' Questions

C. Write an article about "Pet Therapy" using your ideas and addressing the questions from (B).

Pet Therapy

By _____

_____

_____

_____

_____

_____

_____

_____

_____

_____

_____

_____

_____

_____

_____

_____

My Notes

_____

_____

_____

_____

UNIT 2

Organizing Ideas

Canadians and Americans: What Makes Us Different?

People who have visited or lived in North America will often talk about certain differences between Canadians and Americans: Canadians are known to be reserved and understated while their southern neighbours are generally more exuberant. Canadians receive free health care, have ketchup flavoured chips, and say "toque" instead of "beanie", whereas Americans do not. On the other hand, Americans use the non-metric system of measurement and the Fahrenheit system, and have restaurants that cannot be found in Canada.

So, why are we so different from our neighbours to the south? Political events over hundreds of years have shaped our two countries differently. While both countries began as British colonies, the United States fought and won a war of independence from Britain in 1776 and became a republic, whereas Canada remained a part of the British Empire and developed into a constitutional monarchy. Even today, the Queen of England reigns as the Queen of Canada under constitutional law.

Also, the settlement patterns of the two countries differ. In the United States, the west was inhabited by various groups of people heading out on their own in search of free land and the "American Dream". Towns sprung up in the American west, with little government control. In fact, the term "the Wild West" is related to the idea that the American frontier was a place where people could live independently. As the government stepped in to provide the lawful authority of the land, it often had difficulty dealing with this type of individualistic person of the American frontier.

By contrast, the Canadian west was populated under the support of the government from the beginning. In this way, the Canadian population developed into a society that was less "individualistic". It is important not to underestimate the effect of this difference on our societies today.

A. Read the text and answer the questions.

Good writing involves good organization of ideas to make the writing more coherent.

1. Check to show the order in which the text is organized.

Ⓐ In Chronological Order

(events arranged in the order that they occur in the passage of time)

Ⓑ In Spatial Order

(information presented according to its physical location or relationships)

Ⓒ In Topical Order

(events ordered based on the nature of the topics)

Ⓓ In Order of Importance

(ideas arranged from least to most important)

2. What is the main idea of each paragraph?

Paragraph 1 _____

_____

Paragraph 2 _____

_____

Paragraph 3 _____

_____

Paragraph 4 _____

_____

B. Use the cluster map to organize your ideas for an article called "Canadians and Americans: What Makes Us Similar?" that you will write based on topical order.

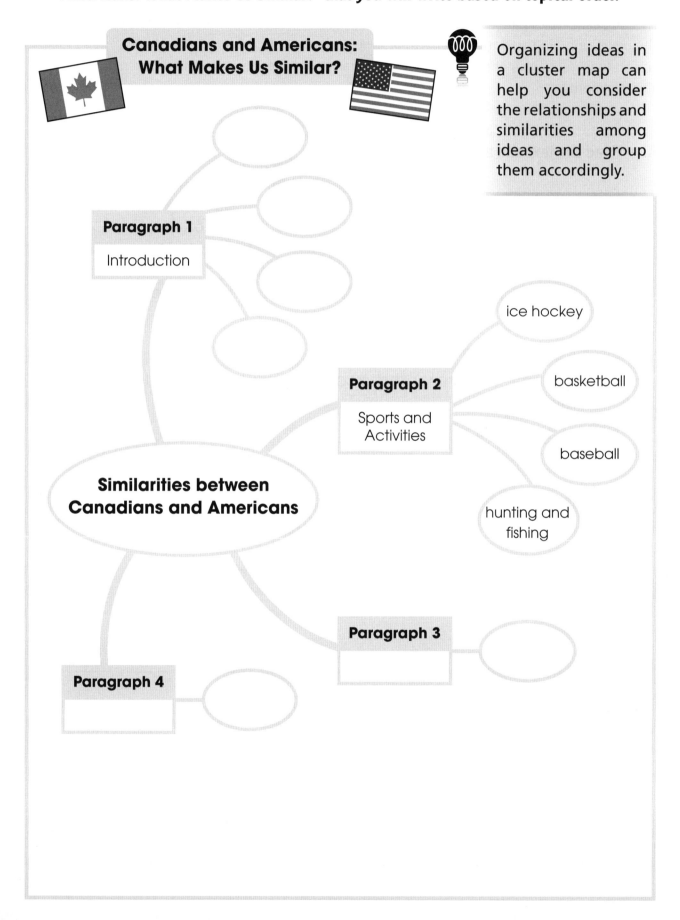

Canadians and Americans: What Makes Us Similar?

Organizing ideas in a cluster map can help you consider the relationships and similarities among ideas and group them accordingly.

Paragraph 1

Introduction

Paragraph 2

Sports and Activities

ice hockey

basketball

baseball

hunting and fishing

Similarities between Canadians and Americans

Paragraph 3

Paragraph 4

C. Write the article "Canadians and Americans: What Makes Us Similar?" using your ideas from (B).

Canadians and Americans:
What Makes Us Similar?

Remember to organize your ideas in a coherent way for the reader.

_____

_____

_____

_____

_____

_____

_____

_____

_____

_____

_____

_____

_____

_____

_____

My Notes

_____

_____

_____

_____

UNIT 3 Third Person Point of View

Bad Luck

Kyle tapped his foot impatiently as he stood under the old oak tree in the schoolyard after class, waiting for his sister, Donna. They were supposed to have left ten minutes ago to meet their friends at the movies, but Donna was nowhere to be seen. *What's taking her so long?* he wondered, growing more and more frustrated. He compulsively checked his phone every couple of seconds to see if she had messaged him. Checking his phone would not help matters, of course, but Kyle was impatient and prone to overreaction.

Donna, meanwhile, was frantically retracing her steps around the school to find her misplaced phone. She knew she was supposed to have left with Kyle over ten minutes ago to meet some friends at the movies, and she knew how impatient her brother could be, but everyone would just have to wait. It was not as if she had planned to lose her phone – she was just having one of those days where nothing was going right! *It's just my bad luck*, she thought miserably. Sighing to herself, Donna began rummaging through her locker for the third time in the vain hope her phone would magically appear somehow.

Mr. Wilson, Donna's Business teacher, who had been watching her search worriedly in every classroom on the second floor, chuckled quietly to himself as he heard her sigh in exasperation. He had found her phone earlier on one of the computer tables in his classroom. She did not notice him as he approached with her phone in hand.

"I think you're missing something, Donna," he said, amused. Donna turned around, wide-eyed as she noticed her phone. Donna thought she might burst with happiness at the sight of it. "Thank you, Mr. Wilson. You're a lifesaver!" she chimed. *If I didn't find it today, I probably would have cried!* she thought. He smiled at her as she hurried away, thinking about how often this happened with students.

But though she hurried, Kyle, impatient as ever, was done waiting. He did not want to be late for the movie, and Donna had a tendency to make everyone late for everything. Sighing, he walked to the bus stop. He did not know of his sister's predicament, of course. If he did, he might have helped her out instead of leaving without her. Instead, he boarded the bus by himself, and Donna, upon approaching the oak tree and noticing her brother was not there, continued wondering why today of all days the universe decided to give her bad luck.

A. **Read the story "Bad Luck" and give an example from the text to show the use of the third person omniscient point of view for each character. Then check the true statements.**

In the third person omniscient point of view, the narrator is a god-like figure that sees all and knows all. The narrator can move between different characters and events and access the thoughts, feelings, and motivations of different characters in a single scene.

Third Person Omniscient Point of View for:

• **Kyle**

   e.g. *What's taking her so long?* he wondered, growing more and more frustrated.

• **Donna**

   e.g. _____

   _____

   _____

• **Mr. Wilson**

   e.g. _____

   _____

   _____

In the third person omniscient point of view, the narrator of the story:

Ⓐ does not use multiple perspectives.

Ⓑ gives opinions and/or makes judgments.

Ⓒ is not a character in the story.

Ⓓ sees and knows things the characters do not.

B.   Read the texts and identify whether they are in the third person objective or omniscient point of view.

Ⓐ   Third Person ＿＿＿＿＿ Point of View

Ⓑ   Third Person ＿＿＿＿＿ Point of View

Ⓒ   Third Person ＿＿＿＿＿ Point of View

Ⓓ   Third Person ＿＿＿＿＿ Point of View

In the third person objective point of view, the narrator shows events as they happen. The narrator can describe what the characters are saying or doing, but cannot access their thoughts or feelings.

Ⓐ   When Jay stepped into the dark alleyway, he felt as though someone were watching him. He could sense someone's presence. He did not usually get scared easily, but he felt his heart race. *Who could it be?* he thought as he quickened his pace, not daring to turn around.

The objective point of view is like a camera – capturing what is external, not internal.

Ⓑ   Cassandra sat alone on the rooftop of her apartment building. The stars were bright above her and she watched them with an awestruck expression. Beside her, her cat purred gently and crawled into her lap. "How bright they are," Cassandra whispered to her cat with a slight smile on her face.

Ⓒ   For as long as he could remember, Ian had loved animals. There was not an animal in need that he would not stop to help. He felt closer to animals than he did to people, and this bothered him. But he should have known it was okay. It meant that no matter how many people left his life, he would never get lonely.

Ⓓ   Selina stood alone in the corner of the banquet hall with a can of soda in hand. She looked as though she were waiting for someone, with the way her eyes kept travelling to the main doors. After a few moments, Selina placed her can on an empty table and left the hall.

C. Rewrite the text in the third person limited point of view, focusing only on Donna's perspective.

Mr. Wilson, Donna's Business teacher, who had been watching her search worriedly in every classroom on the second floor, chuckled quietly to himself as he heard her sigh in exasperation.

> *In the third person limited point of view, the narrator knows the thoughts and feelings of only some (usually one or two) characters, and conveys them through the perspective of a single character at a time.*

He had found her phone earlier on one of the computer tables in his classroom. She did not notice him as he approached with her phone in hand.

"I think you're missing something, Donna," he said, amused. Donna turned around, wide-eyed as she noticed her phone. Donna thought she might burst with happiness at the sight of it. "Thank you, Mr. Wilson. You're a lifesaver!" she chimed. *If I didn't find it today, I probably would have cried!* she thought. He smiled at her as she hurried away, thinking about how often this happened with students.

_____

_____

_____

_____

_____

_____

_____

_____

My Notes

_____

_____

_____

_____

UNIT 4

Word Choice, Tone, and Voice

And They're Off!

It was a sunny Saturday afternoon in High Park, the perfect setting for the race to end all races. Harriet the Hare and Wurtle the Turtle were competing in a race to finally answer the age-old question: does slow and steady really win the race?

Team Wurtle came out dressed in green with Wurtle in the lead. The crowd went wild! Soon after, Team Harriet came out dressed in white. The crowd hooted and hollered excitedly! Wurtle, with his green jersey tied around his shell, let out a little yawn. Harriet, in her little white jersey, twitched her nose in anticipation.

At half past one, the crowd fell silent with suspense. Soon, a bell rang and Harriet hopped quickly forward. Wurtle also began his slow trek toward the finish line.

Suddenly, Harriet stopped in the middle of the track. She perked up, distracted by all the sights and sounds of the park. Wurtle was slowly but steadily making his way toward the finish line. Harriet then took a few more hops forward but stopped again. Then Wurtle overtook Harriet and right before he crossed the finish line, it was as if time was moving in slow motion. The crowd held their breath. When Wurtle finally crossed the finish line, the crowd erupted in cheers!

As the sun set on that lovely Saturday and the crowd began to disperse, one thing was clear as day: slow and steady does indeed win the race.

The Value of Perseverance

By Beaver Bailey

A crowd of hundreds gathered at High Park on Saturday afternoon to witness the race between Harriet the Hare and first-time racer Wurtle the Turtle. A poll conducted by Smart News prior to the race indicated that nearly 95% of the attendees believed Harriet would win the race. To everyone's surprise, it was Wurtle that crossed the finish line first.

A poll was conducted by Smart News.

Sources say that Harriet the Hare started the race off strong, using her speed and agility to outpace Wurtle the Turtle. However, she became distracted and stopped mid-track, while Wurtle, though slow in speed, remained focused on the task.

When asked what Wurtle the Turtle's success meant for his team, one member had this to say: "The outcome of the race proves that success is a matter of perseverance and hard work, not merely natural talent. Indeed, slow and steady did win the race for Wurtle the Turtle."

A. **Read the texts. Then circle the answers and fill in the information.**

1. Word Choice for "And They're Off!":

   descriptive / informative

   Impact of Word Choice:

   _____

   _____

2. Word Choice for
   "The Value of Perseverance":

   descriptive / informative

   Impact of Word Choice:

   _____

Word choice refers to the precise use of vocabulary to establish the writer's voice. Voice is the unique and consistent personality and style of writing.

Appropriate word choice is essential to conveying ideas to the audience in an impactful way.

Section 4

Writing

B. **Read the texts. Circle the tone used and fill in the information. Then answer the questions.**

Voice is also established through tone. Tone conveys the shifting attitude or mood through the choice of words.

A Diana looked out the window with a little smile on her face as she warmly thought of her friend returning home. Diana waited day after day for the letter that would announce the news of her friend's safe arrival. Though it had not arrived yet, it was only a matter of time. Until then, she would watch the soft December snowfall and fondly anticipate a reunion with her dear friend.

Tone	Words to Convey Tone
• (positive) / negative :	smile, warmly, safe, fondly, reunion
• indifferent / hopeful :	_____

B Diana gazed out the window for what seemed like hours, solemnly taking in the sight of the barren fields of white. She gazed into the distance, sighing gravely at the bleak early December landscape. Her thoughts were intent on the question of when her friend would return to town. Day after snowy day she waited for a letter, a phone call, a message – anything that would give her a sign she would not be alone in the cold, desolate winter.

Tone	Words to Convey Tone
• lively / gloomy :	_____
• encouraged / discouraged :	_____

1. In your opinion, which text would lead to a positive outcome for the story? Explain.

   _____

   _____

2. Which authorial voice do you find more appealing? Why?

   _____

   _____

C. Rewrite the text using appropriate words to achieve the tone that you would like to convey.

Jason was home alone and he was very hungry. He went into the kitchen and took out a box of cereal. He opened it and found it empty. Then he put the box into the recycling bin. Jason searched for food all over the kitchen but there was nothing there.

You can replace some words to convey your authorial voice by looking up their synonyms that fit your style! Add other words wherever appropriate.

_____

_____

_____

_____

_____

_____

_____

_____

_____

_____

_____

_____

My Notes

_____

_____

_____

_____

UNIT 5 Rhetorical Devices

Grace's Graduation Speech

Good morning family, friends, faculty, and fellow graduates.

It is an honour for me to be here today as Valedictorian of our graduating class at Oakdale Academy. Can you believe that we're graduating from middle school today? Finished. Done. Finito! I would like to say how proud I am to be a part of this class, and of Oakdale Academy. Today is a bittersweet day, and although some see it as only the end of an era, I want to remind you that it is also a new beginning.

First, to our teachers – you have probably heard this hundreds of thousands of times...but thank you, thank you, thank you! You have been our guiding stars, our compasses, and our mentors. We would not be here without your leadership and support. Thank you for always lending us a hand, an ear, and a shoulder to lean on. Thank you for putting up with us this past year. So, as knights are loyal to the crown, we'll always be loyal to our school.

To our proud parents and families – we thank you for your support. It must be hard to believe that your children will be attending high school next year. But no matter how old we get, we will always be your little big kids.

And finally, to my fellow graduates – we did it! We worked hard and now all of our determination has paid off. Through thick and thin, we have been through it all together – from our first fabulous dance to our final fun field trip.

CONGRATULATIONS!

Our journey to this day has been like a trek through a park. We have tripped and fallen a few times, but we have always got back up. No matter how many times we have been pushed down by bad circumstances, we have managed to rise again. So, remember to always believe that you can achieve great things, and great things will come to you. If you ever feel discouraged, remember to trust yourself. If you ever feel lost, remember that you are not alone. And if you ever feel scared, remember that you are strong and can overcome anything life throws at you!

Our graduation caps and robes represent more than just tonight's graduation event; they represent the beginning of the next chapter in our academic careers.

So, to our terrific principal, teachers, families, and friends – thank you! Enough talking for now... let's celebrate!

A. Write an example from the text for each rhetorical device.

Rhetorical Devices

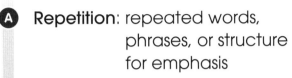
A rhetorical device uses language to convey meaning, emphasize, persuade, or evoke a certain emotion in the audience.

A **Repetition**: repeated words, phrases, or structure for emphasis

B **Hyperbole**: an exaggeration

C **Rhetorical Question**: question asked for dramatic effect rather than to get an answer

D **Oxymoron**: contradicting terms put together

E **Analogy**: explaining one thing by comparing it with another thing

F **Alliteration**: using the same beginning sound in a series of words

Examples from the Text:

A _____

_____

B _____

_____

C _____

_____

D _____

_____

E _____

_____

F _____

_____

B. **Read the text below and write an example for each rhetorical device. Then check the answers.**

> **Rhetorical Devices**
>
> **A** Personification: giving human qualities to non-human things
>
> **B** Metaphor: comparing two things by stating one thing is the other
>
> **C** Simile: comparing two things using the word "like" or "as"
>
> **D** Epistrophe: repeating a word or phrase at the end of successive sentences

The wind sighed through the leaves of the trees as Bruce trekked his way along the dirt path. Early fall weather was perfect for a refreshingly exhausting hike. And as it happened, Bruce decided that he direly deserved the distraction. Lately, he had been sulking around the house like an irritable cat, and it was about time he breathed in the refreshing air of early morning. He had about a million things he needed to do, but everything could wait until tomorrow. His work could wait until tomorrow. Running errands could wait until tomorrow. Answering e-mails could wait until tomorrow. Right now, he was a bird – free and drifting through the air without a care. He was right, wasn't he?

A _____

B _____

C _____

D _____

Which other rhetorical devices are used in this passage?

rhetorical question ☐   alliteration ☐

hyperbole ☐   analogy ☐

oxymoron ☐   repetition ☐

C. **Rewrite the text using as many rhetorical devices as you can to make it more engaging.**

This designer scarf is now on sale! It is handmade in Turkey and is pure silk with intricate beading. It features beautiful colours and a floral design depicting Turkey's official flower, the tulip. It is lightweight and silky soft, perfect for any occasion. Purchase it as a gift for yourself! This sale will not last long so buy it while you still can at this amazing price!

_____

_____

_____

_____

_____

_____

_____

_____

_____

_____

My Notes

_____

_____

_____

_____

UNIT

6 Revising and Proofreading

Books Change Lives

Books change lives – not just for those who learn to read and are inspired by the stories, but sometimes for the subject of a book that is based on a true story. This is exactly what happened to a young Chinese girl named Ma Yan, who lived an anonymous life in a remote village called Zhang Jia Shu, located in the Ningxia region of northern China. Today, Ma Yan is known around the world.

In 2001, Beijing correspondent Pierre Haski, who worked for the French publication "Liberation", was visiting China to film a documentary on Chinese Muslims. He and a group of journalists had visited Ma Yan's boarding school and stayed in the remote village for a few days in a modest hut. While they were there, Ma Yan's mother gave Haski a bundle of Ma Yan's diaries. On them, Ma Yan had written about the hardships she and her family faced. Most of all, Ma Yan had worried that she would not be able to continue her education because her parents could not afford it. On those worn-out pages, Ma Yan went on to mention how her family had to eventually pull her out of school. She hoped that she could continue school so that she could help her family better in the future.

Haski was moved by her writing and offered to help. He gave the family a small gift of money and wrote about their plight in his publication in early 2002. Suddenly, more donations began pouring in. Due to this chance encounter, Ma Yan and her family were pulled out of poverty.

The story was so popular that Ma Yan's diary was translated into French and published in France. It soon became a bestseller. Since then, it has sold over 200 000 copies and has been translated into over a dozen languages. The success of "The Diary of Ma Yan: The Struggles and Hopes of a Chinese Schoolgirl" gave Ma Yan and her family enough money for her schooling and other necessities. Her village has also been given basic necessities such as fresh water and agricultural fertilizers. In addition, in 2002, the fund Children of Ningxia was set up to send children to school.

Thanks to Ma Yan, many Chinese schoolchildren have continued school on the way to a better life. From the influence of Haski, Ma Yan now wishes to be a journalist like "Uncle Han", as she calls him. When asked why she wanted to be a journalist, she answered that she wanted to help poor children around the world like what Uncle Han did for her.

A. **Read the text. Then compare it with its unrevised draft below and write the correct letters to identify the strategies used for revising it. You may use a letter more than once.**

Revision Strategies

 Revising entails checking your work for organization and focus. One effective revision strategy is **ARMS** (add, remove, move, and substitute). When revising, it is also important to fact-check the information in your work.

Ⓐ **A**dd words or sentences.

Ⓑ **R**emove words or sentences.

Ⓒ **M**ove words or sentences.

Ⓓ **S**ubstitute words or sentences (e.g. to revise for facts).

popular Ⓐ
The story was so that Ma Yan's diary was translated into French and published
^

in France. ~~It was published~~. It soon became a ~~Number 1~~ bestseller. Since

200 000
then, it has sold over ~~100 000~~ copies and has been translated into over a

Her   also
dozen languages. (~~Ma Yan's~~ village has been given basic necessities such
^

fresh
as water and agricultural fertilizers.) (The success of "The Diary of Ma Yan:
^

Schoolgirl
The Struggles and Hopes of a Chinese ~~girl~~" ~~also~~ gave Ma Yan and her family

2002
enough money for her schooling and other necessities.) In addition, in ~~2003~~,

children
the fund Children of Ningxia was set up to send to school. ~~The setting up of~~
^

~~the fund Children of Ningxia helped send many children to school.~~

B. **Proofread the texts for grammar, spelling, and punctuation errors. Make corrections above the mistakes.**

Proofreading should take place after revising. Proofreading requires close reading to correct grammar, spelling, and punctuation errors.

Remember, good grammar includes the proper use of verb tense and subject-verb agreement.

1. Books has the powr to change the world. They move us, inspired us; help us connect with each one of us, and make us to see the world in knew ways. Book can instruct, inform, explain, or entertaining us. Books are foods for the soul. Can you think of a time where you got carryed away if reading a good book?

2. Lizzies' faverite kinds of book is a comic book. She is a visualizing learner so the gorgeus art appeals to her. Comic books are about all visualizing meaning in a text: the dynnamic colours the lay out of the panels, the expressive of the lines in theart work together to tell the story. Comic books are just not for kids they are for every one That is why when Lizzie grown up, she wants to be a comicbook writer. and share her love of comic books with the world.

C. Revise and proofread the text. Then rewrite the final draft.

They were sitting by the window huddled together rapped up in a blanket. Thomas remembers his mother read alice's Adventures in Wonderland by C. S. Lewis for him when he was so young on rainy nights. No matter how many times many times she read it to him. He would listen intently as the first time she reads it. Sometime, the best memories are of the simple moments

Remember to fact-check!

_____

_____

_____

_____

_____

_____

_____

_____

_____

_____

_____

_____

My Notes

_____

_____

_____

_____

Science Fiction

The Return of the Sun

It was the year 3081 and it had been nine years since the Earth saw the sun and nine years since humanity started living in Underground City. Due to decades of pollution and humanity's ill-treatment of Mother Nature, the Earth had developed a thick, impenetrable, and unlivable atmosphere of rain and smog. Consequently, the government had ordered everyone to build and live in Underground City, an advanced underground fortress deemed safe and secure from the outside world.

However, today was different. There was a rumour that scientists had predicted that the sun would be seen again on this day. Susan and Bobby, a young, hopeful couple, were incredibly excited. However, the government was quick to squash this rumour.

"We, the government, remind the residents of Underground City that the sun will not be returning today. We repeat, the sun will not be returning today – or ever," said the robotic newscaster.

Despite what the news said, Susan and Bobby were determined to escape Underground City to see for themselves. As no one was allowed outside Underground City, the couple had been planning their escape for weeks. They had their disguises on, their supplies packed, and their route mapped out. Then the two set out on their journey.

When they reached the city limits, they were stopped by robotic guards. The couple lied and claimed to be on a government mission which required going outside the outer limits, but the guards did not believe them. Then, the door accidentally opened just a tiny crack and the couple made a run for it. They ducked past the large, slow-moving guards, boulders, and obstacles, and slid through the door just before it closed again. At the end of the dark tunnel beyond the door, they could see a light.

When they finally reached the end, they climbed out into an open field. It was the most beautiful, green, and lush sight they had ever seen. And the sky, the sky! It was bright blue and dappled with fluffy white clouds. And the best part was the glorious sun. Susan and Bobby basked in its warmth and heat. The sun had not just come out for an hour; the sun must have always been there. Why had the government lied to them?

The couple could hear the sound of guards coming for them, so they ran farther into the field, farther away from Underground City and its government, and into the land of the shining sun.

A. Read "The Return of the Sun" and fill in the information.

Science fiction is a genre of literature in which the story usually takes place in an imagined future full of scientific or technological advancements and major social and/or environmental changes.

1. Setting:

   _____

   _____

   _____

2. Main Characters:

   _____

3. Scientific and Technological Advancement:

   _____

4. Social Change:

   _____

   Environmental Change:

   _____

5. Conflict:

   _____

   _____

   _____

6. Resolution:

   _____

   _____

B.   Fill in the information to brainstorm ideas for a science fiction story that you will write.

> *Scientific and technological advancements can cover topics such as space travel, time travel, aliens, genetic engineering, robots, inter-dimensional travel, and more.*

Title: _____

Theme: _____

Setting

Characters

Scientific or Technological Advancements

Social or Environmental Changes

Conflict

Resolution

C. Write a science fiction story using your ideas from (B). Then draw an image to go with your story.

Title

_____

_____

_____

_____

_____

_____

_____

_____

_____

_____

_____

My Notes

_____

_____

_____

_____

UNIT 8   Film Reviews

"Harry Potter and the Prisoner of Azkaban": Film Review

By Robert Kane | April 14, 2019

"The third film in the series dazzles!"

"Harry Potter and the Prisoner of Azkaban", originally released on June 4, 2004, remains a resounding success. Alfonso Cuarón's admirable adaptation of the third book in J. K. Rowling's epic fantasy series manages to capture the spirit of the original text in a wildly entertaining, two-and-a-half hour ride. "Harry Potter and the Prisoner of Azkaban" moves beyond the lightness of the first two films into a world that has grown more perilous, yet still full of magic and wonder.

The film follows the central character, Harry Potter, a teenage wizard at Hogwarts School of Witchcraft and Wizardry, and his two friends Hermione Granger and Ronald Weasley. Together, the trio attempts to fight off a dangerous fugitive, Sirius Black, who was implicated in the disappearance of Harry's parents and is supposedly intent on confronting him. After escaping from the infamous Azkaban prison, Sirius Black is hunted by the prison's guards, the dementors. These deadly soul-sucking wraiths prove to be fearsome foes for the young wizard.

One of the most captivating aspects of the film is the budding bond between Harry and the new Defense Against the Dark Arts teacher at Hogwarts, Professor Remus Lupin. A friend

of Harry's parents, Professor Lupin becomes a much needed ally to the young wizard as the world around him grows darker. Cuarón adds depth and new emotional layers to the characters through a masterful use of lighting and close camera shots.

The stunning visual effects in the film, such as CGI (Computer Generated Imagery), bring the magic of Hogwarts to life and put the audience right in the centre of the action. Yet, they are never overdone and flashy – they add to the story rather than take away from it. Cuarón manages to build suspense and a looming sense of danger through repeated imagery, such as Sirius Black's sinister wanted poster that appears in several shots throughout the film. Furthermore, the performances by the actors are moving and authentic, and the film's signature music scores heighten the enchanting atmosphere.

Effectively exploring justice, evil, and the power of friendship, "Harry Potter and the Prisoner of Azkaban" is perhaps the best film in the Harry Potter franchise.

A. Read the review of "Harry Potter and the Prisoner of Azkaban" and check the objective features of a film review. Then answer the question.

Objective Features of a Film Review

1. film rating

2. background information (title, director, release date, setting)

3. classification (genre)

4. description of the theme

5. evaluation of the film's strengths and weaknesses

6. identification of cinematic techniques

7. descriptions of plot and characters

8. reviewer's opinion of the film

A film review is a critical evaluation in the form of a descriptive article. The writer of the review gives objective information about the film as well as subjective comments and opinions based on the objective information.

Check to show whether the reviewer's evaluation of the film is positive or negative. Then give examples from the review.

Examples

○ **Positive Evaluation**

1. _____
_____

○ **Negative Evaluation**

2. _____
_____

B.   Write "F" for facts, "PO" for positive opinions, and "NO" for negative opinions.

Example:

Although the <u>visual effects</u> (F) are

<u>stunning</u> (PO), the <u>action sequences</u> (F) are

<u>poorly paced</u> (NO).

> A fair evaluation cannot be made until the reviewer has all the relevant facts and has watched the film to comprehend the plot, acting performances, its technical aspects, and other relevant details.

1.   The <u>stunning</u> ◯ <u>visual effects such as CGI</u> ◯ are <u>never overdone or flashy</u> ◯.

2.   The director <u>effectively builds suspense</u> ◯ through the <u>sound effects</u> ◯, but the <u>camera shots</u> ◯ <u>need improvement</u> ◯.

C.   Fill in the information of a movie you have recently watched for a review that you will write. Then colour the stars to rate it out of five.

Title: _____

Director: _____

Release Date: _____

Genre: _____

Setting: _____

Cinematic Techniques:
(cinema shots, camera angles, etc.)

_____

Description of Plot/ Characters/Themes

Evaluation

☆☆☆☆☆

D. Write a brief film review using the information from (C). Include all relevant objective and subjective information.

Title

_____

_____

_____

_____

_____

_____

_____

_____

_____

_____

_____

_____

REVIEW

My Notes

_____

_____

_____

_____

Section 4

Writing

UNIT 9
School Campaign Flyers

VOTE
VICTORIA
FOR TREASURER

It just makes "cents"!

MISSION: To put the needs of the school and students first

She Supports:

$ balancing the budget through careful spending practices

$ accountability in all financial record keeping

$ encouraging student involvement in the school's financial decisions

$ accessibility of financial education to help students manage their personal budgets

She Will:

$ ensure there are no budget deficits

$ cut out all unnecessary expenditures

$ assist in fundraisers and charity events

$ put the "fun" in fundraisers and be the best treasurer this school has ever seen

$ keep her promises

"**Bank on me!** I'll treasure your vote!"

Count on someone who can count. Vote ***Victoria.***

This is a school campaign flyer for Victoria, who is running for School Treasurer. School campaign flyers tell voters about the individuals running, the positions they are running for, the candidates' mission statements, and their platforms (what they plan to do in the position if elected). The flyers are meant to be distributed widely and should be eye-catching to attract voters. Victoria's campaign flyer has a theme that is related to her desired role.

A. **Write an example from the school campaign flyer for each feature. Then fill in the information.**

Feature	Example
1. Theme	_____
2. Heading	_____
3. Subheading	_____
4. Slogan	_____
5. Mission Statement	_____
6. Platform	_____
7. Quote	_____
8. Image	_____
9. Variety of Fonts	_____

I'm going to photocopy and distribute my flyer so that a lot of people can see it and vote for me.

Victoria can distribute the campaign flyer by:

1. _____

2. _____

3. _____

B. **Imagine you are running for School President. Brainstorm ideas for a campaign flyer that you will create.**

Theme: _____

Heading: _____

Subheadings: _____

Slogan: _____

Mission Statement: _____

Platform: _____

_____

_____

_____

Quote: _____

Images:

An image or picture of the candidate should be placed on his or her campaign flyer.

Additional Features and Content:

_____

_____

_____

C. Create your own campaign flyer using your ideas from (B).

Campaign Flyer for School President

My Notes

_____

_____

_____

_____

UNIT

10 Pie Charts

Brianna's Busy Weekend

This pie chart shows how Brianna spent her time on the weekend.

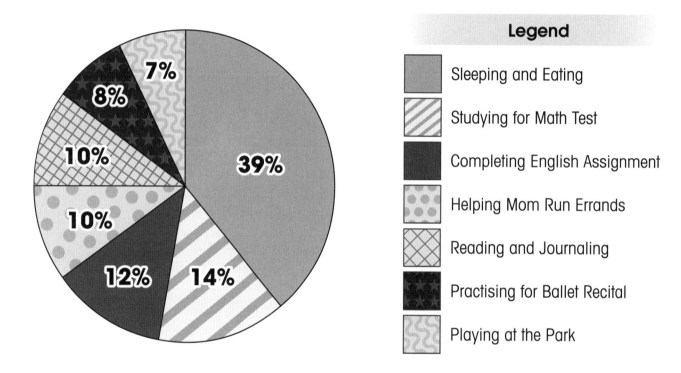

Legend

- Sleeping and Eating
- Studying for Math Test
- Completing English Assignment
- Helping Mom Run Errands
- Reading and Journaling
- Practising for Ballet Recital
- Playing at the Park

A pie chart is a circular statistical graph that shows parts of a whole in order to compare the relationship among the parts and relate each part to the whole. Each part represents a specific category's contribution to the whole. In a pie chart, the sum of all parts is 100%. Also, each part of the data should take up a portion of 360° because a circle has 360°.

To make a pie chart, calculate the total value (for example, the total value is 48 hours in this case). Then divide the value of each part by this total value and multiply by 100 to get a percentage amount. To calculate each angle, divide the percentage amount by 100 and multiply it by 360°.

360°

A. **Look at the pie chart "Brianna's Busy Weekend" and check the features of a pie chart. Then answer the questions.**

1. Features of a Pie Chart:

    (A) two or more categories

    (B) a relevant title

    (C) bars

    (D) an introductory sentence that describes the chart

    (E) overlapping categories

    (F) a scale

    (G) a legend

    (H) a caption

    (I) contains data

    (J) different colours and/or patterns to distinguish categories

    (K) total percentage adding up to 100%

    > Pie charts visually compare data, allowing the reader to comprehend information quickly.

2. Why are colours and/or patterns an important feature of a pie chart?

    _____

    _____

3. Why might having too many categories on a pie chart make it unclear?

    _____

    _____

    _____

4. Do you think a pie chart is an effective way to organize the information shown in "Brianna's Busy Weekend"? Explain.

    _____

    _____

    _____

B. Create a pie chart with the information provided.

Information for Maggie's Pie Chart:

Maggie's monthly budget is spent on rent ($750), savings ($625), groceries ($250), entertainment ($500), and other, which includes pet food and cleaning supplies ($375).

> Include an introductory sentence if you think it will help describe the pie chart.

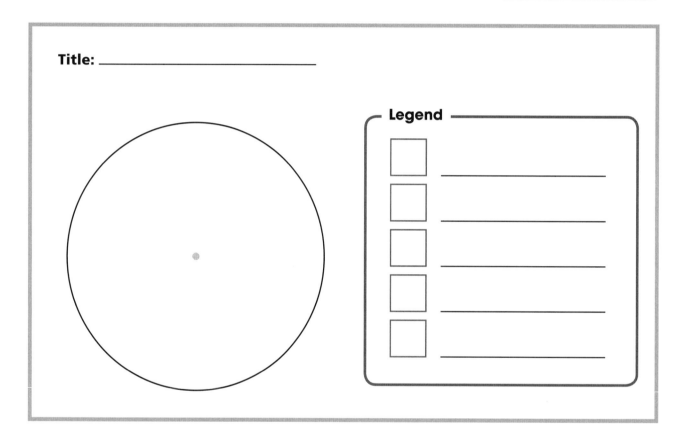

Title: _____

Legend

C. Create your own budget and write down your calculations for a pie chart that you will make.

Information for My Pie Chart

D. **Create a pie chart of your own budget using the information from (C).**

Ask yourself these questions.

- Are there more than two categories?

- Do all the parts add up to 100%?

- Are the colours and/or patterns clear?

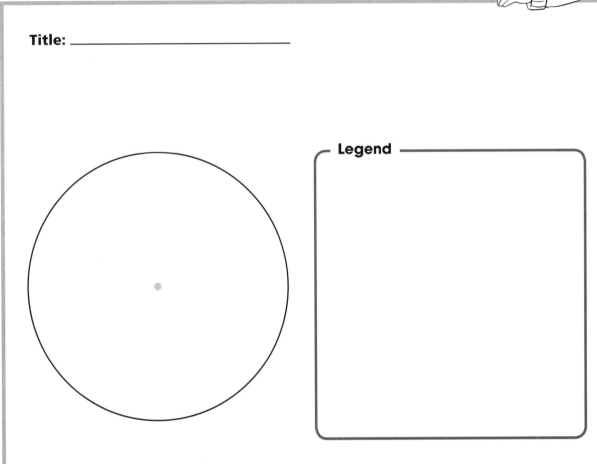

Title: _____

Legend

Writing

My Notes

_____

_____

_____

_____

UNIT 11 — News Scripts

Living with Robots

Good evening, Toronto. My name is Tom Murray and welcome to Smart News. Tonight's story, "Living with Robots", is an in-depth look at life with robots by journalist Anne Harvey. Over to you, Anne.

Thank you, Tom. Living with robots – is this a good or bad thing? Robots are not just used for manufacturing automobiles, dismantling bombs, or building planes. Nowadays, you can find robots in your own home. What is happening in Japan is a good case in point.

Japan has the world's largest aging population, and its birth rate is declining. This means that, in the coming years, there will be a lot of elderly people there and not enough younger people to care for them. The government and the private sector in Japan recognize this as a real problem and are working on ways to deal with it. One innovative solution relates to the manufacturing of robots.

Japan's industrial sector is busy designing robots for use in nursing homes. Robot suits that help the aged stay mobile, and metre-tall speaking robots that act as parent-sitters for grown-up children are some of the items in production. An "automatic washing device", manufactured initially for use in nursing homes, is now finding its place in salons and spas. Now anyone can go to a spa and hop into a machine that offers scented body shampoo and shower, infrared steam, aromatherapy, and even a massage.

Many people are complaining about privacy issues, the resulting laziness, and the possible dangers of malfunctioning robots. However, with new discoveries and technological advancements, avoiding robots altogether is nearly impossible.

So, is living with robots a good thing or bad thing? We will let you decide. Back to you, Tom.

Thank you, Anne, for the insightful report on living with robots. That is all for tonight's news. We hope you found it informative and will let you decide for yourself whether the benefits of using robots outweigh the drawbacks. Signing off, this is Tom Murray with Smart News. Good night.

A. Fill in the information from the text.

A news script is formatted to clearly present information about a specific topic to the public in an unbiased way. It has an opening, transitions, the main news story, and a sign-off. The main news story consists of an introduction, a body, and a conclusion. It answers the 5Ws and the H (who, what, where, when, why, and how).

1. Title:

   _____

2. Opening:

   _____

   _____

   _____

3. Transitions:

   _____

4. Main News Story:

   Ⓐ Introduction: _____

   Ⓑ Body:

   Who: _____

   What: _____

   Where: _____

   When: _____

   Why: _____

   How: _____

   Ⓒ Conclusion: _____

   _____

5. Sign-off: _____

B.　Brainstorm ideas for a news script that you will write.

Title: _____

Remember to focus on a specific topic for the news script.

Intended Audience: _____

Opening: _____

_____

Transitions: _____

Main News Story:

Introduction: _____

_____

Body:

Who _____

_____

What _____

_____

Where _____

_____

When _____

_____

Why _____

_____

How _____

_____

Conclusion: _____

_____

Sign-off

C. **Write a news script using your ideas from (B). Then draw an image for the news.**

Title: _____

_____

_____

_____

SMART NEWS

BREAKING NEWS

_____
_____
_____
_____
_____
_____
_____
_____
_____
_____
_____
_____

My Notes

_____
_____
_____
_____

Section
4

Writing

A. Circle the answers.

1. Defining the audience and purpose of the writing affects its _____.

    form and content

    form and context

    form and comprehension

2. Clustering is a form of _____.

    post-writing

    pre-writing

    pre-revising

3. When clustering, focusing too much on organization may impede the _____.

    pondering of ideas

    free flow of ideas

    plotting of ideas

4. In which type of order are events arranged according to the nature of the subject?

    spatial order

    order of importance

    topical order

5. Chronological order arranges _____.

    ideas from least to most important

    information according to physical location

    events in the order they occur in the passage of time

6. In which point of view can a narrator shift between multiple character perspectives in a single scene?

    third person objective

    third person omniscient

    third person limited

7. Which encompasses the unique and consistent personality and style of writing?

    word choice

    tone

    voice

8. Which conveys the shifting attitude or mood through the choice of words?

    voice

    tone

    word choice

9. A rhetorical device is not used _____.

    to explain

    to emphasize

    to evoke emotion

10. Which rhetorical device repeats a word or phrase at the end of successive sentences?

    epistrophe

    repetition

    alliteration

11. The revision strategy ARMS stands for _____ .

    add, remove, move, and substitute

    add, revise, move, and substitute

    add, remove, move, and shift

12. When revising, it is important to _____ .

    check for grammar

    check for spelling

    fact-check

13. One element of proofreading is _____ .

    adding new words and sentences

    checking for punctuation errors

    rearranging words and sentences

14. A science fiction story usually takes place in _____ .

    an imagined past

    an imagined future

    an imagined present

15. Which topic would likely not be covered in a science fiction story?

    time travel

    mythological creatures

    aliens

16. A film review is a _____ evaluation in the form of a/an _____ article.

    critical ; descriptive

    critical ; instructive

    constructive ; descriptive

17. Which is not an objective feature of a film review?

    descriptions of plot and characters

    identification of cinematic techniques

    evaluation of the film's strengths and weaknesses

18. A pie chart is a circular _____ .

    statistical pie

    statistical graph

    statistical board

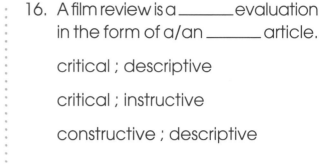

19. Which is not a feature of a pie chart?

    a relevant title

    a legend

    a scale

20. Which is not a feature of a news script?

    transitions

    a slogan

    a sign-off

B.   Read the text and answer the questions.

A New Adventure

Anne and Cleo had gone to the same school since they were in kindergarten. Rain or shine, they would walk together in the mornings, eat their lunches together in the afternoons, and ride the bus home together in the evenings. Anne could not remember a time when these things were not true; she could not remember a time when she and Cleo were not best friends.

Come graduation at the end of the year, the simple things that had become such important parts of their lives were what Anne realized she was going to miss the most. She had also taken for granted that Cleo might not go to the same high school as hers. Either way, they would both have full schedules and time would no longer seem so free and giving. Who knew when she would even get to see Cleo?

"Earth to Anne," Cleo said, waving a hand in front of Anne's face, which had twisted into a tense and troubled expression. "You've been quiet. What's wrong?"

Anne began to tell her it was nothing and that she was fine, but all her thoughts came rushing out like a tidal wave. "It's just...we're graduating soon, and then we'll be attending humongous high schools with millions of students and we'll have metric tons of homework every day. And... we won't get to see each other as much," Anne said dejectedly. "I'm just not ready for Grade 8 to end."

Cleo looked thoughtful as Anne's words settled between them. "Remember what Ms. Symes told us? 'Life is a novel and the end of one chapter is also the beginning of another. A new adventure awaits at the turn of every page.' Anne, we can't let the fear of change hold us back from enjoying this new adventure. And besides, just because we won't see each other all the time doesn't mean we'll stop being best friends," she smiled. "We'll have the weekends and summers, and we can call each other any time!"

Anne smiled; the slow and sorrowful sinking feeling from before was silently slipping away. Cleo was right. Change was often hard, but it helped to know that she was not alone in facing it. Anne and Cleo had the rest of the year to look forward to, their graduation party to look forward to, and the splendid stretch of the summer sun to look forward to. And though she was a little nervous about attending high school in the fall, she was also excited. It would be a new adventure that she and Cleo would share – an unforgettable one.

1. Check the answers and fill in the information.

Type of Word Choice

☐ descriptive

☐ informative

Examples

Verb: _____ _____

Adjective: _____ _____

Adverb: _____ _____

Tone

☐ despairing and doomed

☐ moving and hopeful

Words to Convey Tone:

_____

_____

_____

2. Write the rhetorical device for each example. Then write an example from the text for each rhetorical device.

Rhetorical Device   **Example**

Ⓐ _____ : Who knew when she would even get to see Cleo?

Ⓑ _____ : Anne smiled; the slow and sorrowful sinking feeling from before was silently slipping away.

Ⓒ _____ : ...all her thoughts came rushing out like a tidal wave.

Ⓓ Metaphor: _____

_____

Ⓔ Hyperbole: _____

_____

_____

Ⓕ Epistrophe: _____

_____

_____

_____

C.   **Check the features of a school campaign flyer. Then create a school campaign flyer for Anne to support her candidacy for the President of the Graduation Party Planning Committee.**

Features of a School Campaign Flyer

(A) theme

(B) heading

(C) subheadings

(D) graph

(E) slogan

(F) mission statement

(G) platform

(H) statistics

(I) quote

(J) image

(K) variety of fonts

Vote _____ for

President of the Graduation

Party Planning Committee

Mission Statement: _____

Platform:

"   "

_____

D. Write a school news script about a memorable graduation party. You may use one of the topic ideas to help you.

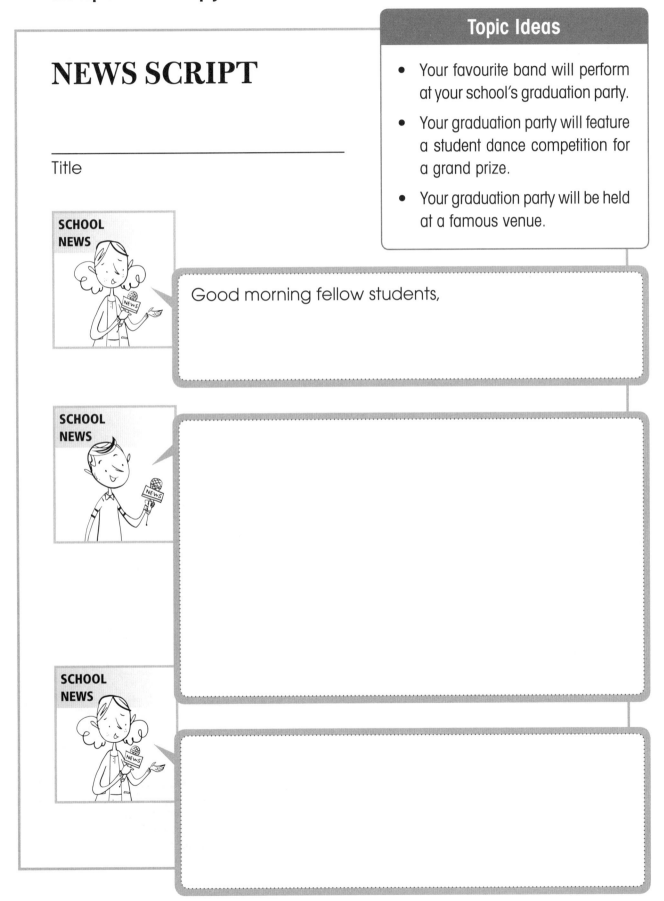

NEWS SCRIPT

_____
Title

Topic Ideas

- Your favourite band will perform at your school's graduation party.
- Your graduation party will feature a student dance competition for a grand prize.
- Your graduation party will be held at a famous venue.

SCHOOL NEWS

Good morning fellow students,

SCHOOL NEWS

SCHOOL NEWS

1.1   A Cross-Canada Culinary Tour

Canada is a vast country with many distinct regions based on geography, political boundaries, and people's ethnic make-up. Naturally, this diversity has a significant impact when it comes to food. While it may be easy for us to think of a national dish for Scotland (haggis), Japan (sushi), or Italy (spaghetti), it is difficult to imagine a food that exemplifies Canada. Instead, what we find, when we go from coast to coast, is a wide and delicious assortment of regional specialties. So, let's take a cross-Canada culinary tour.

If you partake of a home-style meal in Newfoundland, you will certainly find yourself tucking into baked codfish and blueberry pie. If you find yourself eating a lobster supper in a church basement, you could be in Nova Scotia or Prince Edward Island. Fiddlehead soup? These funny greens may have been picked in New Brunswick. If your baked bean casserole tastes a little sweet, with a hint of maple, then you are in Quebec. And if someone hands you a carton of French fries covered in brown gravy and cheese curds, don't back away! This French-Canadian dish is called poutine and is especially popular in Ottawa. If bannock appears on your bread plate and Saskatoon-berry pie is the dessert, then you may be in Saskatchewan.

If someone offers you a perogy, take it! You are now in western Canada – and you could very well be in the province of Manitoba, whose large Polish and Ukrainian populations introduced this food to our country more than a hundred years ago. Perogies are mashed potatoes and cheese stuffed inside a pocket of dough, but don't let the simple ingredients fool you into thinking that the dish is boring. Perogies are boiled, pan-fried, or deep fried, and usually eaten with sour cream, butter, and onions – comfort food at its yummiest! And if barbecued steak and buffalo burgers are on the menu, then welcome to Alberta, Canada's "cattle country".

After all your dining adventures, you may be feeling a bit full – but there's more! Head to Vancouver, British Columbia for the best Chinese and South Asian food in Canada. You can sip jasmine tea and eat dim sum in the hustle and bustle of Chinatown, or try an assortment of Thai spring rolls or Vietnamese rice paper wraps at Granville Island Market...unless, of course, you want to try the catch of the day – fresh wild Pacific salmon.

Canada is an immigrant nation. The truth is, it would not be too hard to find a world of cuisine in any large Canadian city. So dig in!

1.2

1. What food best represents Nova Scotia or Prince Edward Island?
    A. lobster
    B. barbecued steak
    C. bannock
    D. rice paper wraps

2. Where would you likely find fiddlehead soup in Canada?
    A. in Saskatchewan
    B. in New Brunswick
    C. in Prince Edward Island
    D. in Ottawa

3. Which dish is especially popular in Ottawa?
    A. rice paper wraps
    B. baked bean casserole
    C. sushi
    D. poutine

4. Who introduced perogies to Canada a hundred years ago?
    A. the French and the Polish
    B. the Polish and the Ukrainian
    C. the Ukrainian and the Chinese
    D. the Chinese and the Vietnamese

2.1 Surprising Stories about Sound

While you are enjoying your favourite music on your personal audio player, have you ever wondered about the mechanics of hearing? In order to understand how we hear, we must understand the dynamics of sounds and the features of the human ear.

Sound is a series of vibrations, and our ears decode these vibrations for us. First, the part of the ear we can see – the pinna (also called the auricle) – collects the sound vibrations in the air. These vibrations travel down the ear canal to the eardrum. The eardrum vibrates, and three "ear bones" (also called the ossicles) that consist of the hammer, anvil, and stirrup magnify these vibrations. The vibrations then move to the cochlea, the part of the inner ear that resembles a snail shell. The sensory cells inside the cochlea detect the vibrations and change them into messages. Finally, the messages are sent along the auditory nerve to the brain, giving us the sounds we hear.

For most of us, our sense of hearing works so well that we do not consider how limited human hearing is compared to that of animals. Elephants, for example, can communicate at sound levels as low as five hertz. This means that if you flap your hands back and forth faster than five times a second, an elephant can actually hear the tone produced.

The behaviour of animals before earthquakes and other natural disasters gives us an indication of their superior hearing. For example, in 2004, a deadly tsunami, caused by an earthquake on the ocean floor, hit the coastlines of several countries around the Indian Ocean, causing the deaths of over 200 000 people. Surprisingly, most animals in the national parks and zoos in these regions were reported to be unharmed. In Thailand, the elephants that were being used to carry tourists escaped, if they could manage, to higher ground long before the tsunami struck. The elephants were able to sense the vibrations of the earthquake through their feet, and they reacted instinctively by heading uphill. Moreover, the animals – even the local birds in trees – were able to detect the low frequency sound vibrations from the incoming tsunami.

The frequency of a sound refers to the number of vibrations per second. The human ear can hear sounds with a frequency between 20 and 20 000 hertz. As we age, we gradually lose the ability to hear high frequency sounds. With this in mind, a clever inventor developed a tone with a frequency of 17 000 hertz. This tone, called the "Mosquito" tone, has been utilized by convenience store owners to disperse young people lingering around the premises while leaving adult customers unaffected. This technology was given the dubious distinction of an "Ig Nobel Prize" (a spoof of the Nobel Prize).

2.2

1. What does the pinna do?
   A. detects sound vibrations
   B. collects sound vibrations
   C. magnifies sound vibrations
   D. decodes sound vibrations

2. What type of sound vibrations does a tsunami produce?
   A. high frequency sound vibrations
   B. mid frequency sound vibrations
   C. low frequency sound vibrations
   D. a combination of high and low frequency sound vibrations

3. What does the frequency of sound refer to?
   A. a series of vibrations
   B. the number of vibrations per second
   C. the range of hearing ability
   D. the number of tones the human ear can hear

4. What is the range of frequency that the human ear can hear?
   A. between 5 and 17 000 hertz
   B. between 20 and 20 000 hertz
   C. between 20 and 200 000 hertz
   D. between 17 000 and 20 000 hertz

3.1 The World of Tea

After water, tea is the second most-consumed beverage in the world and it has been enjoyed for centuries. Tea production began in China but soon spread to other parts of Asia. When European explorers, such as Marco Polo, came across the satisfying beverage on their travels, they sparked a demand for tea worldwide that has continued to grow, in spite of the competition from soft drinks and coffee.

There are four main types of tea: black, white, green, and oolong. The difference depends on the processes used for treating the tea leaves, such as oxidation, fermentation, heating, and drying. Black tea is withered, fully oxidized, and dried, and makes a strong, amber-coloured brew. English Breakfast and Darjeeling are popular black teas. Green tea is not oxidized; it is withered and then dried. It has a pale green or golden colour and a delicate taste. Oolong tea is between black and green tea in oxidation level and the resulting colour and taste. Very popular in China, oolong is often referred to as the "Champagne of Teas". Don't drink it with milk, sugar, or lemon! White tea is the least processed. It is withered and dried by steaming.

China and Japan produce the best green teas, Taiwan is known for its oolong tea, and India and Sri Lanka are famed for their black teas. Kenya, Argentina, and Vietnam are also major tea producers. The addition of spices, fruits, and flowers can also create different kinds of teas with unique flavours. In recent years, a market niche has been developed for "herbal teas" – chamomile and peppermint are popular – but these are not true teas as they do not derive from the plant Camellia sinensis.

Different regions have their own specialties. For example, Indian masala, or "chai" tea, is made with cardamom, ginger, cinnamon, fennel, and cloves. Mint tea is consumed in North Africa and the Middle East. Bubble tea, especially popular in Hong Kong, Taiwan, and Singapore, is tea mixed with cold milk and dollops of sweet, jelly-like tapioca balls. Earl Grey tea, named after a British prime minister who lived from 1764 to 1845, is the most popular black tea in the world after English Breakfast tea. It is a blend of black teas mixed with bergamot oil. Matcha, made from bright green tea leaf powder, is the staple of the world-renowned Japanese tea ceremony. But now you can get it at popular coffee chains. It is high in vitamins A, B, C, E, and K.

Flowering tea is a novelty tea made by sewing the leaves and flowering parts of tea plants into tight pod-like balls. When the pod is placed in hot water, it opens up, revealing the lovely flower inside.

Versatile and healthful, tea deserves its place as one of the world's most beloved beverages. Let's lift our cups and have a toast – to tea!

3.2

1. Which are examples of popular black teas?
   - A. oolong and masala
   - B. bubble tea and matcha
   - C. English Breakfast and Darjeeling
   - D. peppermint and chai

2. Which type of tea is the least processed?
   - A. black tea
   - B. white tea
   - C. green tea
   - D. oolong tea

3. Which countries are famed for their black teas?
   - A. China and Japan
   - B. India and Sri Lanka
   - C. Kenya and Vietnam
   - D. Taiwan and Argentina

4. What type of tea is chamomile tea?
   - A. black tea
   - B. white tea
   - C. green tea
   - D. herbal tea

4.1 Another "Ice Age" on the Way?

Today, many of the world's scientists and environmentalists are talking about global warming: the gradual and inexorable increase in the world's overall temperature due to increased carbon dioxide emissions and the resulting greenhouse effect. So it may seem odd that many of these same scientists and environmentalists are saying that global warming may bring about another ice age. How can this be?

Scientists refer to the time from about 1300 to 1870 – when temperatures in parts of northern Europe and North America fell – as The Little Ice Age. Although the drop in temperature was only about 1°C, it caused significant hardship. For example, glaciers in Norway advanced onto farmland and caused crop failures in other parts of Europe, leading to famine and starvation. This indicates just how much damage could be caused if temperatures drop more steeply and more quickly – as they did during a much greater ice age 8200 years ago.

Scientists have theorized about this period of rapid cooling, which lasted about 150 years. We can still find evidence of this ice age today: the frozen bodies of woolly mammoths encased in the permafrost of Siberia. One plausible theory for this has to do with the warming effect of the Gulf Stream in the Atlantic Ocean, combined with the demise of North America's glacial reservoir, Lake Agassiz.

The Gulf Stream refers to a current of water in the Atlantic Ocean that moves up along the coast of North America to the North Atlantic Basin. This current begins with warm water from the tropical southern regions of the ocean, which cools and sinks as it heads north. The current then heads south again along the ocean floor, acting like a conveyor belt in a global system of ocean currents. The effect of this current of warm water is very powerful, helping to explain why certain islands along the coast of Scotland have palm trees and why the climate of Iceland is relatively mild despite its high latitude.

It has been theorized that Lake Agassiz, which covered much of inland North America (Lake Winnipeg is a remnant of that ancient inland "sea"), was drained when the Laurentide Ice Sheet located in northeastern North America collapsed. Vast amounts of cold, fresh water began spilling into the warmer, salty Atlantic Ocean, causing the Gulf Stream "conveyor belt" and its warming effect on northern Europe to cease. While some scientists do not agree with this theory, it is important to remind ourselves that the glaciers of Greenland are melting at an unprecedented rate. If this continues, it may disrupt the Gulf Stream and cause another ice age.

4.2

1. Why is the world's overall temperature increasing?
   A. because of increased carbon dioxide emissions
   B. because of melting glaciers
   C. because of the Gulf Stream's heating effect
   D. because of the collapse of the Laurentide Ice Sheet

2. Which areas did The Little Ice Age affect?
   A. Asia and Africa
   B. Europe and North America
   C. Scotland and Iceland
   D. Siberia and Greenland

3. Which is evidence of an ice age?
   A. global warming and the greenhouse effect
   B. crop failures around the world
   C. the collapse of the Laurentide Ice Sheet
   D. frozen bodies of woolly mammoths in Siberia's permafrost

4. What does the Gulf Stream act like?
   A. a greenhouse
   B. a conveyor belt
   C. a glacial reservoir
   D. a remnant of an inland sea

5.1 Special Olympians

For millions of people around the world, the Olympic Games are an exciting and greatly anticipated event. Whether it is winter or summer, the world unites every two years in admiration of the world's greatest athletes. We remember the names of many of them, even those whose achievements occurred over half a century ago: Jesse Owens, who won four gold medals for the United States at the Berlin Olympics in 1936; "the Flying Dutchwoman" Fanny Blankers-Koen who, as a 30-year-old mother of two, won four gold medals at the London Olympics in 1948, and Richard Fosbury, who revolutionized the high jump by jumping over the bar backward at the 1968 Olympic Games. His "Fosbury Flop" soon became the conventional method of clearing the bar. Tessa Virtue, Scott Moir, Patrick Chan, Christine Sinclair, and Clara Hughes are just a few of Canada's famed medal-winners in recent years.

But here are the names of some Olympians you may not have heard of: three-time medal-winner Tahir Ahmed, from Pakistan; three-time medal-winner Latisha Ferguson, from the Bahamas; three-time medal-winner Amita Shrestha, from Nepal. These athletes all participated in the Special Olympics.

The Special Olympics is an international organization that helps people with intellectual disabilities become physically fit and compete at the elite level in an international forum. It was founded in 1968 by Eunice Kennedy Shriver, a sister of former American president John F. Kennedy. The first event was held in Chicago, Illinois that same year. In addition to the Special Olympics World Summer and Winter Games, which alternate every two years, the Special Olympics provides athletic training for more than 5 million athletes in over 170 countries. Athletes must be at least eight years old to participate, and be identified by an agency or a professional as having intellectual disabilities, cognitive delays, or significant learning or vocational problems due to cognitive delays.

Children and adults who participate in the Special Olympics develop improved physical fitness and motor skills, greater self-confidence, and a more positive self-image. They grow mentally, socially, and spiritually. They also enjoy the rewards of friendship and ultimately discover not only new abilities and talents but also their "voices".

The Special Olympic Games are usually held after the Olympic Games. Next time you finish cheering for the great Olympic athletes of the summer or winter games, remember to find the channel that broadcasts the Special Olympic World Games – and keep on cheering!

5.2

1. When did the Fosbury Flop become the conventional high jump style?
   A. before the 1936 Olympics
   B. before the 1948 Olympics
   C. at the 1948 Olympics
   D. after the 1968 Olympics

2. How many medals did Amita Shrestha win at the Special Olympics?
   A. two
   B. three
   C. four
   D. five

3. Who founded the Special Olympics?
   A. Eunice Kennedy Shriver
   B. John F. Kennedy
   C. Jesse Owens
   D. Latisha Ferguson

4. Where was the first Special Olympics event held?
   A. in Berlin, Germany
   B. in Chicago, Illinois
   C. in London, England
   D. in the Bahamas

R1.1 The Rafflesia – a True Floral Wonder

Everyone loves flowers. From the tiniest sprig of honeysuckle that heralds spring with its familiar scent to huge, dripping bouquets of tropical blooms that can fill a room with heady fragrance, there is a flower to suit every preference. But there is one flower that is not likely to please anyone – and what a pity, too, as it is the largest flower in the world!

The Rafflesia, named after Sir Thomas Stamford Raffles, a British explorer and administrator, and the founder of the city of Singapore, was "discovered" – or rather, documented in English for the first time – in 1818 in the rainforest of Indonesia during a research excursion by British naturalist Dr. Joseph Arnold.

This huge flower can only be found in Southeast Asian countries including Indonesia, Malaysia, Thailand, and the Philippines. The most striking thing about the Rafflesia, and its more than 15 different species, is not its size, however. It is its putrid smell! A Rafflesia in bloom gives off an odour akin to rotting meat or even human decomposition. It is not surprising that the name of this flower in local languages translates as "meat flower" or "corpse flower". It is believed that the smell serves an important purpose, however: to attract the flower's pollinators, such as flies and beetles.

The Rafflesia is a parasitic plant; it depends on another plant to thrive and grow. The Rafflesia has no stem, no leaves, and no roots, which makes it necessary for the flowering plant to adhere itself onto another plant, the Tetrastigma vine. The vine has special fungus-like tissue that provides nutrients for the Rafflesia, enabling it to grow to its enormous size. With the five petals in its bloom, mostly red in colour with white spots, the flower can grow to a size of 106 centimetres in diameter and can weigh as much as 10 kilograms. Despite its size and strength, the Rafflesia's life is short-lived. It takes about a year for the flower to grow to its full size, at which point it will start to bloom. The flower stays in bloom for only about a week before dying.

In spite of its odour, nature enthusiasts, as well as tourists, visit the rainforests of Southeast Asia to see the Rafflesia in bloom, and to smell the famous odour for themselves. So famous and rare is the flower that when a Rafflesia growing in the botanical garden of any city around the world begins to bloom, the event is likely to merit a word or two in the local news!

The Rafflesia is the official state flower of Sabah in Malaysian Borneo and the official provincial flower of Surat Thani in Thailand. However, mainly due to increased human activity and habitat loss, all known species of the Rafflesia are either threatened or endangered. Steps are being taken in some Southeast Asian countries to protect the largest and one of the rarest flowers in the world.

R1.2

1. Who was Sir Thomas Stamford Raffles?
   A. a British explorer and naturalist
   B. an Indonesian explorer and naturalist
   C. a British explorer and administrator
   D. a Singaporean explorer and administrator

2. Where was the Rafflesia documented in English for the first time found?
   A. in the city of Singapore
   B. in the rainforest of Indonesia
   C. in the rainforest of Singapore
   D. in the botanical garden in Malaysia

3. What is believed to be the purpose of the strong smell of the Rafflesia?
   A. to attract naturalists
   B. to attract tourists
   C. to attract its pollinators
   D. to be named the official flower

4. For how long does the Rafflesia stay in bloom?
   A. about one week
   B. about one month
   C. about ten months
   D. about one year

Answers

1 A Cross-Canada Culinary Tour

A. 1. A   2. B
    3. A   4. D

B. 1. A   2. B
    3. D   4. B

C. 1. geography
    2. diversity
    3. assortment
    4. Quebec
    5. Vancouver, Bristish Columbia
    6. Poutine

D. (Suggested answers)
    1. Canada does not have one food specialty because of the diversity of people's ethnic make-up due to Canada being an immigrant nation. This leads to Canada having a wide and delicious assortment of regional specialties.
    2. Perogies are the food specialty of Manitoba, introduced by its large Polish and Ukrainian populations more than a hundred years ago. A perogie is a pocket of dough stuffed with mashed potatoes and cheese. It can be boiled, pan-fried, or deep fried, and is usually eaten with sour cream, butter, and onions.
    3. (Individual answer)

E. (Individual summary)

2 Surprising Stories about Sound

A. 1. D   2. C
    3. B   4. D

B. 1. B   2. C
    3. B   4. B

C. 1. T   2. T
    3. T   4. F
    5. F   6. F

D. (Suggested answers)
    1. First, the pinna collects the sound vibrations in the air. These vibrations travel down the ear canal to the eardrum, which vibrates, and three "ear bones" serve to magnify these vibrations. These magnified vibrations move to the cochlea, which detects and changes them into messages. Finally, these messages are sent along the auditory nerve to the brain, giving us the sounds we hear.
    2. Yes, animals can hear better than humans. They can hear much lower sound frequencies than humans. For example, elephants can communicate at sound levels as low as five hertz. They can even hear the tone produced if you flap your hands back and forth faster than five times a second.
    3. (Individual answer)

E. (Individual summary)

3 The World of Tea

A. 1. D   2. D   3. B   4. D
B. 1. C   2. B   3. B   4. D
C. 1. herbal tea   2. bubble tea
    3. mint tea   4. Earl Grey
    5. oolong   6. chai

D. (Suggested answers)
    1. Tea production began in China and soon spread all over Asia. European explorers then discovered it and sparked a worldwide demand for tea that has continued to grow.
    2. Black tea is withered, fully oxidized, and dried; green tea is withered and dried, but not oxidized; oolong tea is slightly oxidized, and white tea is withered and dried by steaming, but not oxidized.
    3. Flowering tea is the leaves and the flowering parts of tea plants sewn together into pod-like balls. When the pod is placed in hot water, it opens up to reveal the flower inside.

E. (Individual summary)

4 Another "Ice Age" on the Way?

A. 1. C
2. A
3. B
4. C

B. 1. A
2. B
3. D
4. B

C. 1. global warming
2. glaciers
3. crop failures
4. Siberia
5. Lake Agassiz
6. Lake Winnipeg
7. melting
8. mild

D. (Suggested answers)
1. Scientists believe that when Lake Agassiz was drained when the Laurentide Ice Sheet collapsed, vast amounts of cold, fresh water spilled into the warmer, salty Atlantic Ocean, causing the Gulf Stream "conveyor belt" and its warming effect to cease, which resulted in the drop in temperatures.
2. The Gulf Stream is a current of water in the Atlantic Ocean that moves up along the coast of North America to the North Atlantic Basin. This current begins with warm water from the tropical southern regions of the ocean, which cools and sinks as it heads north. It then heads south again along the ocean floor, acting like a conveyor belt in a global system of ocean currents, thereby having a warming effect on certain geographical areas.

E. (Individual summary)

5 Special Olympians

A. 1. A
2. C
3. C
4. A

B. 1. D
2. B
3. A
4. B

C. 1. T
2. T
3. T
4. F
5. F
6. T
7. T
8. F

D. (Suggested answers)
1. The Special Olympics is an international organization that helps people with intellectual disabilities become physically fit and compete at the elite level in an international forum.
2. Athletes who are at least eight years old and identified by an agency or a professional as having intellectual disabilities, cognitive delays, or significant learning or vocational problems due to cognitive delays can participate in the Special Olympics.
3. Athletes who participate in the Special Olympics develop improved physical fitness and motor skills, greater self-confidence, and a more positive self-image. They grow mentally, socially, and spiritually. They also enjoy the rewards of friendship and discover not only new abilities and talents but also their "voices".

E. (Individual summary)

Review 1

A. 1. largest
   2. 1818
   3. Southeast Asian
   4. more than 15
   5. parasitic plant
   6. the Tetrastigma vine
   7. five
   8. about one year

B. 1. C
   2. B
   3. C
   4. A

C. 1. T
   2. T
   3. F
   4. T
   5. F
   6. F

D. 1. documented the Rafflesia in English for the first time in 1818
   2. is its putrid smell, which is akin to rotting meat or even human decomposition
   3. that provides nutrients for the Rafflesia, enabling it to grow to its enormous size
   4. that when it blooms in the botanical garden of any city around the world, the event is likely to merit a word or two in the local news

E. 1. The flower can only be found in Southeast Asian countries including Indonesia, Malaysia, Thailand, and the Philippines.
   2. The smell of the Rafflesia attracts the flower's pollinators, such as flies and beetles.
   3. Despite its size and strength, the Rafflesia's life is short-lived.
   4. Nature enthusiasts, as well as tourists, visit the rainforests of Southeast Asia to see the Rafflesia in bloom.
      (Individual writing)

F. rainforest ; Indonesia ; Rafflesia ; largest ; putrid ; smell ; meat ; corpse ; Southeast ; Asian

G. (Check these statements.)
   1. The Rafflesia's petals are usually red with white spots.
   2. The Rafflesia can grow up to 106 cm in diameter.
   3. The Rafflesia can weigh up to 10 kilograms.

H. (Suggested answers)
   1. The Rafflesia is a parasitic plant with no stem, leaves, or roots, which makes it necessary for it to adhere itself onto another plant, the Tetrastigma vine, to thrive and grow.
   2. The Tetrastigma vine has special fungus-like tissue that provides nutrients for the Rafflesia, enabling it to grow to its enormous size.
   3. All known species of the Rafflesia are either threatened or endangered mainly due to increased human activity and habitat loss.

I. (Individual summary)

1 Prepositional and Phrasal Verbs

A. (Suggested answers)
1. to   2. to
3. at   4. about
5. with   6. to
7. at   8. of
9. to   10. at
11. on

B. 1. believed in
2. vowed to ; speak to
3. rely on
4. joke about
5. apologized for
6. pretended to ; laughed at
7. disagreed with
8. cares about
9. hear about
10. dreamed about ; going to

C. 1. put out
2. figure out
3. look up
4. keep up with
5. give away
6. call off
7. came up with
8. broke into

D. 1a. B   b. A
2a. A   b. B
3a. A   b. B
4a. B   b. A

E. (Individual sentences)

F. 1. into   2. for
3. for   4. from
5. on   6. for
7. on   8. up for
9. off   10. on
11. down   12. off
13. on   14. out
15. up
Prepositional Verb: 1, 2, 4, 6, 7, 10, 13
Phrasal Verb: 3, 5, 8, 9, 11, 12, 14, 15

2 Finite and Non-finite Verbs

A. 1. ✔   2. ✘   3. ✔   4. ✔
5. ✘

B. 1. walks ; agreement   2. stopped ; tense
3. stayed ; tense   4. are ; agreement
5. have ; agreement

C. 1. winning   2. trapped
3. barking   4. excited
5. inspiring   6. Speeding
7. promising   8. refreshing
9. finished   10. giggling
11. stolen ; deserted 12. entertaining

D. 1. Recycling ; S   2. Laughing ; S
3. writing ; O   4. hiking ; O
5. cooking ; O

E. 1. Jumping over the ditch can be dangerous.
2. He sustained a severe injury as a result of falling.
3. Losing in the eighth inning upset the game plan.
4. Increasing the use of fuel leads to more pollution.

F. (Suggested answers)
1. To forgive   2. to sleep
3. to complete   4. To succeed
5. to celebrate   6. to exercise
Infinitive as a Noun: 1, 2
Infinitive as an Adjective: 3, 6
Infinitive as an Adverb: 4, 5

3 Non-progressive Verbs

A. 1. am seeing ; see
2. are smelling ; smell
3. Are you hearing ; Do you hear
4. is not feeling ; does not feel
5. are feeling ; feel
6. was hearing ; heard
7. is not tasting ; does not taste
8. was seeing ; saw
9. were feeling ; felt
10. was tasting ; tasted
11. is smelling ; smells

B. 1. likes   2. need
   3. preferred   4. appreciate
   5. hates   6. wished
   7. loves   8. delighted

C. (Suggested sentences)
   1. My best friend has moved to Edmonton and I miss him very much.
   2. Clare did not give up although she feared her opponents.
   3. The task seems impossible but I wonder if there is a solution.

D. 1. believe   2. forgets
   3. imagine   4. doubt
   5. realized   6. suppose
   7. thinks   8. recognized
   9. agreed   10. remembers
   11. believes

E. 1. has   2. belongs
   3. includes   4. contains
   (Individual sentences)

4   Modal Verbs

A. 1. (cannot) ; see ; ability
   2. (should) ; try ; suggestion
   3. (could) ; give ; request
   4. (could) ; have ; possibility
   5. (can) ; play ; permission
   6. (should) ; look ; advice
   7. (may not) ; be ; possibility
   8. (will) ; take part in ; certainty

B. (Suggested answers)
   1. You: Mr. Torres, may we ask some more questions?
      Mr. Torres: Yes, you may.
   2. You: Could I borrow a pencil, Elena?
      Elena: Here you go. You can use this one.
   3. You: Could you give me a ride home, Mrs. Ross?
      Mrs. Ross: Yes, of course. You may sit in the passenger seat.
   4. You: Mom, can I please watch the baseball game?
      Your mom: Sure, you can watch it after this show ends.

C. (Individual answers)

D. 1. If you play in the sun, you should wear a cap.
   2. Since there is no school tomorrow, we could go to the movies.
   3. May I adopt a dog from the animal shelter?
   4. ✔
   5. You may leave your bag in my office.
   6. Everyone must help keep the classroom tidy.
   7. ✔
   8. Jessica can speak English, French, Spanish, and Japanese.

5   Order and Position of Adjectives

A. 1. new ; age
      white ; colour
      running ; purpose
   2. favourite ; opinion
      blue ; colour
      ceramic ; material
   3. popular ; opinion
      young ; age
      British ; origin
   4. handsome ; opinion
      brown ; colour
      leather ; material
   5. big ; size
      round ; shape
      dining ; purpose
   6. sparkling ; opinion
      heart-shaped ; shape
      diamond ; material
   7. charming ; opinion
      petite ; size
      French ; origin
   8. small ; size
      old ; age
      wooden ; material

B. A: sparkling, small, oval

B: beautiful, old, medieval

C: soft, pink, woollen

D: witty, lanky, Canadian

E: dazzling, huge, red

F: handy, new, gardening

1. D   2. A   3. B   4. F

5. E   6. C

C. (Individual sentences)

D. 1a. B   b. A

2a. A   b. B

3a. A   b. B

4a. B   b. A

5a. B   b. A

E. (Individual sentences)

6   Correlative Conjunctions

A. 1. Whether ; or

2. Neither ; nor

3. either ; or

4. Not only ; but ; also

5. whether ; or

6. not only ; but also

7. Neither ; nor

8. either ; or

B. 1. E   2. A   3. C   4. C

5. D   6. A   7. B   8. E

9. B   10. D

C. 1. their   2. their

3. her   4. his

5. his   6. their

7. their   8. her

9. his   10. their

D. 1. ✗ ; Neither he nor his friends are good at playing basketball.

2. ✗ ; Either you or Jack has to pay for the broken window.

3. ✔

4. ✗ ; Neither Wendy nor her sisters know how to drive.

5. ✗ ; Either my friends or I am going to prepare snacks for the outing.

7   Conditional Clauses

A. 1. it turns to ice

2. if we are tired or sick

3. there is no school

4. they are ready to eat

5. all cars stop

6. if it rains

7. if my alarm clock does not work

8. if he has given it to you

B. 1. is ; will stand

2. will make ; give

3. will find ; keep

4. agree ; will be

5. travels ; will go

6. will achieve ; works

7. are ; will be

8. rains ; will cancel

C. (Individual answers)

D. 1. If Devon came, he would bring his pet dog with him.

2. They would invite you if you were a committee member.

3. If we were denied entry, we would have our gathering somewhere else.

4. If I were the teacher, I would teach my students how to make telescopes.

5. Max would make a candy castle if he had millions of candies.

6. If Jen stayed at the party, Fran would be very happy.

7. Karen would save the planet if she had superpowers.

8. If I owned a spaceship, I would fly to other planets.

E. 1. The team would have lost if Derek had not hit a homerun in the ninth inning.

2. We would have stopped if he had warned us.

3. If Rachel had been more supportive, the team would have been able to make it.

4. If Dad had shown them the pass, he would not have been charged.

5. If the gate had been locked, the animals would not have run away.

8 Dependent Clauses as Nouns, Adjectives, and Adverbs

A. 1. that he needed his parents' permission before going on a vacation with his friends ; O
2. Whatever you do ; S
3. Whether or not they could make it ; S
4. Where the robbers are hiding ; S
5. which train passed by the little town ; O
6. how they would get to the city ; OP
7. whichever movie you pick ; OP
8. whoever comes first in the race ; OP

B. 1. (whom I met today)
2. (that we had last night)
3. (where I bought my new shoes from)
4. (that my grandma knitted for me)
5. (that Jenny recommended him to read)
6. (which Tracy accidentally dropped)

C. (Individual sentences)

D. 1. ✔   2. ✔
3. ✔   4. ✘
5. ✔   6. ✘

E. (Individual sentences)

F. 1. where he thought the treasure was buried
2. that he knew the code
3. Whichever road you take
4. who scored the winning run
5. how we can improve ourselves as individuals
6. whose hat was red
7. before the soccer game could even begin
8. until we could see the first ray of the morning sun
9. whom everyone can trust
10. because some of their family friends came to visit them
11. What Ken wants to know ; how he can join the basketball team
12. that she wished to get
Noun Clause: 2, 3, 5, 11
Adjective Clause: 4, 6, 9, 12
Adverb Clause: 1, 7, 8, 10

9 Inversion

A. 1. Was he able
2. Were they going
3. Has Ella been volunteering
4. Will Grandpa and Grandma visit
5. Can Benny take
6. Are Neelu and Jessie
7. Will Jessica be going

B. 1. B
2. A
3. A
4. B
5. B
6. A

C. 1. Lizzie taller, she would be allowed on the roller coaster
2. they bought the tickets earlier, they would have saved some money
3. you require more details, please visit our website
4. Had we practised more together, we would have won the game.
5. Should you want to participate in the event, please sign up by the end of June.
6. Had Jenna been correct, we would all have received a surprise gift.
7. Were Harry the chairperson, he would definitely turn down the proposal.
8. Were Mrs. Clark to run the marathon, we would all run with her.

D. (Suggested writing)
here:
Here come Mr. and Mrs. Rivera with their baby.
Here stands a hundred-year-old tree.
there:
There goes the little kitten after the squirrel.
There stood the statue of a mermaid in the middle of the fountain.

10   Voice and Mood

A. 1. The fire was put out in less than an hour.

2. The annual meeting will be held as scheduled.

3. A baby whale was seen off the shore.

4. The pamphlets were handed out to all the Grade 8 students by the teacher.

5. All borrowed books should be returned to the library before noon today.

6. Janet was awarded The Student of the Year Award by the principal.

B. 1. P   2. A   3. P   4. A

   5. P   6. P   7. A   8. P

   9. A

Rewritten in the Active Voice:

1 ; Grade school children enjoy dodge ball as a fun game.

3 ; The players outside the circle throw a big, rubber ball and aim it at the players inside the circle.

5 ; The players can only throw the ball

6 ; If a player throws the ball

8 ; If the ball hits a player in the circle

C. 1. IND   2. IMP   3. IND

   4. IMP   5. IND   6. IND

D. 1. Do not waste any more time on the minor details.

2. Please contact Mrs. Jones on my behalf.

3. Buy it online if you want to save time.

4. Bear right when you see the sign "Snowview".

E. (Individual sentences)

11   Ellipses and Dashes

A. (Suggested answers)

1. There was a flash of lightning and then... thunder.

2. I was going to leave but...I heard a strange noise.

3. Josh went to the store...and came back with two bags of groceries.

4. Stella dreamily sighed...

5. The committee...is proud to present the award to Jacob Stubbs.

6. Anna walked in...and screamed as everyone cried, "Surprise!"

B. 1. I will eat broccoli – so long as it is covered in cheese.

2. She ran to the park – or rather, she leaped to the park.

3. There are only three things Tim is afraid of – thunder, heights, and loneliness.

4. All four girls – Jenna, Marilyn, Rebecca, and Kristina – made the honours list.

5. He would only leave his house during the winter for one thing – pizza.

6. My brother hates three things – country music, rock music, and line dancing.

7. Ruby called Dr. Crowley – her family doctor – on Monday to schedule an appointment.

C. 1. Samuel Langhorne Clemens was a famous American writer ‸ better known by his pen name Mark Twain.

2. Mark Twain ~~has written "The Adventures of Tom Sawyer", "Adventures of Huckleberry Finn", "Life on the Mississippi", "The Prince and the Pauper", and "A Tramp Abroad" and~~ ‸ is often referred to as the father of American literature.

3. When Twain was four, his family moved to Hannibal ‸ ~~(a port town on the Mississippi River)~~ where he was inspired to write "Adventures of Huckleberry Finn".

4. Ernest Hemingway ‸ another famous American writer ‸ is best known for his novel "The Old Man and the Sea".

5. In 1920, Hemingway took a job at ~~a newspaper in Toronto~~ ‸ the Toronto Star.

6. Many critics touted Hemingway's "A Clean, Well-Lighted Place" ‸ a short story ‸ as one of the best stories ever written.

7. To be a good writer ~~(I have concluded after interviewing 12 writers)~~ ‸ is to write clearly and concisely.

8. I have a wish ‸ to be as great and successful as the famous Mark Twain and Ernest Hemingway one day.

D. (Individual sentences)

Answers

Review 2

A. 1. I depend on you.
   2. It agrees with the subject in number.
   3. gerund
   4. feel, see, smell, believe
   5. possession
   6. modal verb
   7. May I borrow your car?
   8. The wise old English teacher smiled.
   9. cotton – material
   10. either...or
   11. Neither Julia nor Robert knew where his money was.
   12. It is used for general truths.
   13. third conditional sentence
   14. You cannot donate it to whomever you choose.
   15. Rarely do I go out anymore.
   16. Had you been there, you would have laughed.
   17. They could not wait for their turn.
   18. –

B. a. phrasal
   b. finite
   c. non-progressive
   d. prepositional
   e. non-finite
   1. set out
   2. to progress
   3. realized
   4. shut down
   5. to learn
   6. given
   7. inspiring
   8. read over
   9. believe in
   10. listening
   11. challenging
   12. want
   13. have
   14. weighed
   15. approve of

C. young, school-going
   well-established educational
   huge, deserted
   personal knowledge
   1. not only
   2. but also
   3. No sooner
   4. than
   5. Not only
   6. but
   7. also
   8. as many
   9. as

D. First Conditional Sentence: 3
   Second Conditional Sentence: 4
   Third Conditional Sentence: 1
   Dependent Clause as a Noun: 5
   Dependent Clause as an Adverb: 7 ; 8
   Dependent Clause as an Adjective: 2 ; 6

E. 1. A   2. B   3. A

F. Before the governor could say another word,
   Active Voice
   voices of agreement rose up throughout the hall.
   Active Voice
   Julian's wise words had caused a massive uproar
   Passive Voice
   and the listeners were moved by his impassioned speech.

   After hours of deliberation – much of which were spent by an apprehensive Julian sitting on the edge of this seat – the governor finally came to the decision that the boy who had voiced his opinion was...right!

   The governor went on to elaborate that although technology was powerful, it could not replace social interaction and individual learning.
   Passive Voice
   Traditional education could not be replaced by knowledge chips.

   That fall, knowledge chips were recalled as schools reopened. Julian smiled to himself as he walked through the doors of his bustling new high school.

1   Harry's Dream

A. 1. Harry   2. Harry's dad and friends
   3. to act   4. at the end of the year
   5. He saw a poster for a casting call.
   6. the drama teacher
   7. excited
B. (Suggested answers)
   1. The message of the short story is that it is important to do what is right for you and follow your dreams, regardless of what anyone else says.
   2. The conflict Harry faces is physical. He faces the conflict that his father and friends are not initially supportive of his dream to be an actor because he is good at basketball, which is more popular. This initially discourages Harry from auditioning for the school play.
   3. (Individual answer)
C. C ; A ; D ; E ; B
D. (Suggested answer)
   Similarity:
   Harry acts in the play.
   Harry's father and friends watch him perform in the play.
   Harry's father and friends like his performance in the play.
   Harry decides to pursue acting.
   Difference:
   Harry's father and friends tell Harry not to pursue acting and to focus solely on basketball.
   Harry is troubled because he lacks the support of his father and friends even after the play.
   Harry hopes one day his father and friends will support him.
   Harry is content rather than happy.
   This ending does not give the story a proper resolution.

2   Two Kingdoms

A. 1. strong but ruthless
   2. at night in Tom's room
   3. Tom and his friend Jim
   4. stormy   5. his father's sword
   6. the sounds of battle 7. in the morning
   8. to speak to the king of the other kingdom
B. (Suggested answers)
   1. Tom cares about his kingdom and the people in it, as is shown when he says, "I long for the days of peace and prosperity, when children can go out and play on the streets without fear". Tom is also determined and strong-willed, as is shown when he asserts that he will visit the other king and request a peace treaty to end the fighting once and for all.
   2. Tom's kingdom has lost its prosperity and has been largely destroyed by an ongoing battle with another kingdom. It has lost all of its cattle and crops, and people are starving. The kingdom is no longer peaceful and prosperous.
   3. Tom is worried and anxious about visiting the king of the other kingdom because he feels that something terrible will happen to him there, such as being captured. Yet, he is hopeful that the king of the other kingdom will accept his request for a peace treaty.
C. (Check these points.)
   is written in poetic form.
   follows a rhyme scheme.
   tells us that the play is about two opposing kingdoms.
D. (Check these elements.)
   metaphor ; foreshadowing ; one speaker
   (Suggested answers)
   1. The soliloquy shows that Tom is deeply troubled by the ongoing conflict between the two kingdoms and is determined to find a way to end it, despite his apprehension about meeting the other king.
   2. The soliloquy foreshadows something bad because Tom uses negative language to describe the weather, the battle, and his father's sword. He also says that he has a foreboding feeling that something terrible will happen to him if he visits the other kingdom.

3   Junk Food Is Good Food

A. 1. the brain   2. F.A.K.E.
   3. Faculty of Advanced Kitchen Eating
   4. head of J.O.K.E.
   5. Mr. Swee Tuuth
   6. on online forums
   7. because of an abundance of toxins, fatty acids, and external chemicals

B. (Suggested answers)
   1. The purpose of this article is to criticize online forums that claim to provide factual information with no scientific evidence to back it up, as well as people who try to argue that consuming unhealthful foods is not bad for you.
   2. The intended audience of this article is people who easily believe anything they read online without verifying the information. This article criticizes their lack of judgment and teaches the audience to not believe whatever they read without questioning it.
   3. (Individual answer)

C. (Suggested examples)
   Irony: A new study has been done by junk food enthusiasts which concludes that eating excessive amounts of fatty, sugary, and oily junk food is indeed healthful for you after all.
   Exaggeration: ..."but as a fellow lover of good, greasy food, I can say this discovery is a true scientific breakthrough...without all the actual science, of course."
   Parody: When asked if his team at F.A.K.E. could supply us with an approximated illustration of the chemical structure of the nutrient "junk", Dr. Sill Ypants merely said that studying the supposed nutrient was "not a priority at this time".

D. (Individual answers)

4   Ms. Day's Class Survey

A. 1. reading habits
   2. Ms. Day's Grade 8 students

3. The students' names will not be shown.
4. 35
5. visualize the descriptions
6. Most students in the class love reading.

B. 1. The purpose of this survey is to assess the reading habits of Ms. Day's Grade 8 class so that Ms. Day can learn more about the class and better cater to its needs.
   2. (Individual answer)
   3. A ; B ; B

C. (Suggested writing)
   A. Do you think reading is a good habit?
   B. Do you enjoy reading textbooks?

D. (Individual answers)

5   Canadian English Thesaurus

A. 1. Canadian English Thesaurus
   2. finding the synonyms of words
   3. B
   4. adjective
   5. The word "scream" has its own word entry number.
   6. three

B. (Suggested answers)
   A: to list all the word entries in the thesaurus so that users can easily look up the synonyms of words
   B: to indicate the first or last word entry on the page
   C: to show the user the location of the word they want to find the synonym of
   D: to distinguish between different uses of a word
   E: to show the word entry being looked up
   F: to indicate that the word also has its own entry in the thesaurus as well as being a synonym of the word it is placed under

C. 1. responsible   2. bland
   3. coat   4. explosion
   5. burst   6. blatant
   7. comprehensive   8. bleary

D. C ; E ; F
   (Individual synonyms)

6   Water Pollution

A. 1. the contamination of water bodies
   2. when pollutants are discharged into water bodies
   3. soil erosion
   4. burning of fossil fuels
   5. contaminated drinking water
   6. using fertilizers and pesticides

B. 1. ✗   2. ✔
   3. ✔   4. ✗
   5. ✔   6. ✗
   7. ✔

C. 1. (Individual answer)
   2. (Suggested answer) People use fertilizers and pesticides on their lawns and gardens, and these products seep into the groundwater and ultimately into larger water bodies. These water bodies become polluted, which has various negative effects such as the death of aquatic animals.
   3. (Individual answer)

D. Definition: B
   Causes: D
   Effects: A, E
   Solutions: C, F

7   Just Like Grandma Used to Make – A Memoir by Mia

A. 1. Mia and her grandma
   2. Mia
   3. cherry pie
   4. on special occasions
   5. the tapping of their shoes as they danced
   6. dearie
   7. vanilla ice cream
   8. love and care

B. (Suggested answers)
   1. Mia's grandmother was her best friend as she was growing up and was the person who inspired her to become a chef, so their relationship is very significant for Mia.
   2. 1. Make the crust by mixing all the ingredients together and then roll and shape the dough with your hands.
      2. Place the dough in the pan.
      3. Pour in the cherry filling.
      4. Bake the pie in the oven. When the timer goes off, remove the pie from the oven.
      5. Top it off with a scoop of vanilla ice cream.

C. (Suggested sentences)
   1. She was the one who inspired me to become a chef.
   2. Whenever we baked her famous pie, we would play smooth jazz music in the background.
   3. On special occasions, like when I received a good mark at school, my grandma would make my favourite dessert – cherry pie.
   4. I loved cooking with my grandma. She was the best chef, even better than my mom, but I would never tell my mom that.
   5. Of course, I will never be as good as my grandma, but I hope to make her proud and keep her memory alive.

D. (Suggested answer)
   The text shows that Mia's grandmother loved Mia and enjoyed making cherry pies with her. Mia and her grandmother had a lot of fun making cherry pies together – they would listen to jazz music and dance together in their matching aprons. When Mia tried stealing cherries, her grandmother swatted her hands away playfully without hurting her feelings. Mia's grandmother also nudged her playfully out of the way to take the pie out of the oven carefully, as she made it for Mia to enjoy. Out of concern for Mia, she then lovingly warned her not to eat it while it was too hot as Mia might burn her mouth. Mia's grandmother also called Mia "dearie", which shows the affection she had for her.

8   Springville High School Student Transcript

A. 1. four   2. Date of Birth
   3. 30   4. 16 years old
   5. Independent Study
   6. French and English
   7. 2018 – 2019
   8. 12

B. 1. student number
   2. cumulative G.P.A.
   3. community hours
   4. grade level
   5. credit
   6. principal's signature
   7. percentage grade

C. (Suggested answers)
   1. John Smith: to make informed decisions about his academic future
     John Smith's Basketball Coach: to determine John's physical education performance
     Springville High School's Student Counsellor: to advise John on his academic future and/or career options
   2. The features of this transcript that set it apart from another school's transcript include the school name, school logo, and the principal's name and signature.

D. (Suggested answers)
   1. John's grades in all of his courses except for Music went up, demonstrating that he improved his knowledge and abilities in almost all of his courses. For example, his grade in English went from 75% to 77%. His grade in Music remained the same high grade of 85%, showing that he always performed strongly in that course. John did well in Physical Education in Grade 9, but did not take it again in Grade 10.
   2. English: 75 ; 77 ; 85 ; 88
     Math: 78 ; 79 ; 85 ; 88
     French: 77 ; 79 ; 83 ; 87
   (Individual answer)

9   Beppu, Japan

A. 1. World Travel Magazine
   2. its *onsen*
   3. in Kyushu
   4. healing properties
   5. orange red
   6. at Takegawara Spa

B. (Suggested answers)
   1. The purpose of this online magazine article is to encourage travel enthusiasts to visit Beppu, Japan.
   2. Travellers interested in geothermal energy or people who want to relax on vacation might be the intended audience because the article highlights how Beppu, Japan provides points of interest for both.
   3. Japan has so many hot springs because it is located atop shifting tectonic plates, and is therefore a site of frequent earthquakes and geothermal activity.
   4. (Individual answer)

C. 1 O
   2. F
   3. F
   4. O
   5. F
   6. O

D. B ; C ; D ; E ; F ; G ; H
   (Individual writing)

10 Stress Management

A. 1. all the employees at Smart Company
   2. harmful
   3. a rise in heart rate
   4. insomnia
   5. in the afternoon of December 6
   6. in the main conference room
   7. articles on stress management
   8. the president

B. (Suggested answers)
   1. The purpose of this memo is to inform the employees of the negative effects of stress, ways to reduce and manage stress, and to announce a de-stress session.
   2. Short paragraphs and bullet points are used in the memo to allow for quick reading and easy access to information.
   3. The memo is written objectively.
   4. (Individual answer)
   5. Mr. Wright is representing Smart Company as he is sending out a memo to all Smart Company employees because he is the president of the company.
   6. Header: The header includes the recipients, the sender, the date, and the subject line.
      Introduction: The introduction explains that it is a busy time of year when the holidays and year-end deadlines can cause stress to employees, and that the memo is to provide tips to manage it.
      Body: The body explains how stress negatively affects the body and suggests ways to reduce and manage stress. It also announces the de-stress hour and that employees can request further information on stress management.
      Conclusion: The conclusion reminds the employees that the company cares about them. It also advises employees to reach out to the Human Resources Department for further assistance.

C. (Individual writing and drawing)

11 WeConnect

A. 1. the most recent
   2. Comment, share, and like it.
   3. by group and friend
   4. a telescope
   5. local school
   6. the principal
   7. by date
   8. on May 6 at 3:30 p.m.

B. D ; E ; A ; B ; G ; C ; F

C. (Suggested answers)
   1. The purpose of the social networking website is to allow students and teachers at the school to connect online and share relevant information.
   2. The students and teachers at the school with access to WeConnect would use this website.
   3. (Individual answer)

D. 1. (Individual answer)
   2. (Individual writing)

Review 3

A. 1. exposition, rising action, climax, falling action, resolution
2. at the opening
3. a character's speech to himself or herself
4. humour
5. to inform
6. unbiased questions
7. synonyms
8. legend
9. problem, definition, causes, effects, solutions
10. arrows
11. Memoir
12. first person point of view
13. principal's signature
14. the student's school counsellor
15. an attention-catching graphic element
16. A fact can be proven true or false.
17. its subscribers
18. to entertain
19. home page
20. in the search bar

B. 1. False
2. True
3. True
4. False
5. True
6. False
7. False

C. (Suggested answers)
1. The moral of the short story is to take on one task at a time and to remain calm rather than trying to do everything at once and getting overwhelmed.
2. psychological ; The conflict that Rider faces is that he becomes stressed out about all of the work that he has to complete, and this stress makes it difficult for him to get the work done efficiently.

3. The resolution of the story is that Rider steps back to re-evaluate how he is handling his work. He decides to change his approach and tackle one task at a time, which allows him to reduce his confusion and get all of his work done on time.
4. (Individual answer)

D. (Suggested answers)
1. The purpose of this satire is to show how obstructive procrastination is to success by making it clear how ridiculous it is to claim that procrastination is the key to success.
2. The intended audience of this satire is people who procrastinate and do not think that it is a bad thing to do.
3. Irony: ...procrastination, and not hard work, is the key to success after all!
   Exaggeration: And isn't that what every working person wants – to be thinking about work every waking hour of the day?

E. 1. A
2. D
3. C
4. E
5. F
6. B

(Suggested answers)
7. The main purpose of this memo is to remind employees not to use their work hours for personal matters.
8. Bullet points are used to make it easier for readers to know which parts of the memo are the most important for them to read, and to present the information concisely.
9. This memo is written objectively because no individuals are mentioned and the company uses facts to prove its point, including examples of what some employees are doing when they should be working, as well as how much money is being lost daily due to the decreased productivity of the employees.

1   Developing Ideas

A. (Suggested answers)

1. The intended audience is people looking for ways to de-stress.

2. to explain ; to inform

3. The topic is music as a form of therapy and a way to de-stress.

4. (Suggested facts)

- Cave dwellers fashioned musical instruments from animal bone.

- When a person listens to music, his or her brain releases dopamine, a neurotransmitter that makes him or her feel good and happy.

- Music and its therapeutic qualities have become an important element in nursing homes, hospitals, and rehabilitation centres.

5. (Individual question)

B. (Individual writing)

C. (Individual writing)

2   Organizing Ideas

A. 1. B

2. (Suggested writing)

Paragraph 1:

Canadians and Americans differ in many ways.

Paragraph 2:

Canadians and Americans differ due to historic political events that shaped the two countries in very different ways.

Paragraph 3:

The settlement patterns of the two countries and their level of government control had significant impacts on their people.

Paragraph 4:

Canadian society is less "individualistic" than American society because Canada had more government support from the beginning than America.

B. (Individual writing)

C. (Individual writing)

3   Third Person Point of View

A. (Suggested examples)

Donna: *It's just my bad luck*, she thought miserably.

Mr. Wilson: He smiled at her as she hurried away, thinking about how often this happened with students.

(Check these letters.)

C ; D

B. A: omniscient

B: objective

C: omniscient

D: objective

C. (Suggested writing)

"I think you're missing something, Donna," Donna heard someone behind her say. She turned around and saw that it was Mr. Wilson, her Business teacher. Wide-eyed as she noticed her phone in his hand, Donna thought she might burst with happiness. "Thank you, Mr. Wilson. You're a lifesaver!" she chimed. *If I didn't find it today, I probably would have cried!* she thought as she hurried away.

4   Word Choice, Tone, and Voice

A. 1. descriptive ;

Impact of Word Choice: (Suggested answer) Readers are able to visualize the race in great detail.

2. informative ;

Impact of Word Choice: (Suggested answer) Readers get the important information they are looking for without too much detail.

B. A: hopeful ;

(Suggested words) returning ; waited ; announce ; arrival ; Until ; anticipate ; reunion

B: gloomy ;

(Suggested words) solemnly ; barren ; sighing ; gravely ; bleak ; alone ; cold ; desolate discouraged ;

(Suggested words) hours ; when ; waited ; anything ; sign ; alone

1. (Individual answer)
2. (Individual answer)

C. (Individual writing)

---

5   Rhetorical Devices

A. (Suggested examples)

A: Thank you

B: First, to our teachers – you have probably heard this hundreds of thousands of times...

C: Can you believe that we're graduating from middle school today?

D: little big kids

E: Our journey to this day has been like a trek through a park. We have tripped and fallen a few times but we have always got back up.

F: Through thick and thin, we have been through it all together – from our first fabulous dance to our final fun field trip.

B. (Suggested examples)

A: The wind sighed through the leaves and trees as Bruce trekked his way along the dirt path.

B: Right now, he was a bird – free and drifting through the air without a care.

C: Lately, he had been sulking around the house like an irritable cat, and it was about time he breathed in the refreshing air of early morning.

D: His work could wait until tomorrow. Running errands could wait until tomorrow. Answering e-mails could wait until tomorrow.

(Check these rhetorical devices.)

rhetorical question ; alliteration ; hyperbole ; oxymoron ; repetition

C. (Individual writing)

---

6   Revising and Proofreading

A. The story was so ^popular(A) that Ma Yan's diary was translated into French and published in France. ~~It was published(B)~~. It soon became a ~~Number 1(B)~~ bestseller. Since then, it has sold over ~~100 000~~ 200 000(D) copies and has been translated into over a dozen languages. (~~Ma Yan's~~ Her(D) village has also(A) been given basic necessities such as ^fresh(A) water and agricultural fertilizers.)⌒(C)(The success of "The Diary of Ma Yan: The Struggles and Hopes of a Chinese ~~girl~~ Schoolgirl(D)" (B) ~~also~~ gave Ma Yan and her family enough money for her schooling and other necessities.) In addition, in ~~2003~~ 2002(D), the fund Children of Ningxia was set up to send children(A) to school. ~~The setting up of the fund Children of Ningxia helped send many children to school.(B)~~

B. 1. Books have the power to change the world. They move us, inspire us, help us connect with one another, and make us see the world in new ways. Books can instruct, inform, explain, or entertain us. Books are food for the soul. Can you think of a time when you got carried away while reading a good book?

2. Lizzie's favourite kinds of books are comic books. She is a visual learner so the gorgeous art appeals to her. Comic books are about visualizing meaning in a text – the dynamic colours, the layout of the panels, and the expressive lines in the artwork together tell the story. Comic books are not just for kids; they are for everyone. That is why when Lizzie grows up, she wants to be a comic book writer and shares her love of comic books with the world.

C. Thomas and his mother were sitting by the window, huddled together and wrapped in a blanket. Thomas remembered his mother reading "Alice's Adventures in Wonderland" by Lewis Carroll to him on rainy nights when he was young. No matter how many times she read it to him, he would listen as intently as he did the first time she read it. Sometimes, the best memories are of simple moments.

7   Science Fiction

A. (Suggested answers)
  1. The setting is in the year 3081, when the world has been destroyed by humanity's ill-treatment of the Earth and people are living in an underground fortress called Underground City, where they cannot see the sun.
  2. Susan and Bobby
  3. advanced underground fortress and robots
  4. Social Change: Humans are forced to live underground and robots live among humans. Environmental Change: The Earth has developed a thick, impenetrable, and unlivable atmosphere of rain and smog due to pollution and humanity's mistreatment of nature.
  5. The government insists that the sun will never come out, and humans are forced to remain in the underground fortress. However, Susan and Bobby do not believe the government and plan to see the sun for themselves.
  6. Susan and Bobby escape Underground City and realize that the sun has, in fact, always been there. Thus, they decide to stay away from Underground City.
B. (Individual writing)
C. (Individual writing and drawing)

8   Film Reviews

A. 2 ; 3 ; 4 ; 6 ; 7

Positive Evaluation
  1. "Harry Potter and the Prisoner of Azkaban", originally released on June 4, 2004, remains a resounding success.
  2. The stunning visual effects in the film, such as CGI (Computer Generated Imagery), bring the magic of Hogwarts to life and put the audience right in the centre of the action.
B. 1. PO ; F ; PO
   2. PO ; F ; F ; NO
C. (Individual writing)
D. (Individual writing)

9   School Campaign Flyers

A. 1. money
   2. Vote Victoria for Treasurer
   3. She Supports:
   4. It just makes "cents"!
   5. Mission: To put the needs of the school and students first
   6. balancing the budget through careful spending practices
   7. "Bank on me! I'll treasure your vote!"
   8. Victoria
   9. The title and platforms are written in different fonts.
   (Individual answers)
B. (Individual writing and drawing)
C. (Individual writing and drawing)

10   Pie Charts

A. 1. A ; B ; D ; G ; I ; J ; K
   (Suggested answers)
   2. Colours and patterns help readers quickly identify the different categories shown by the pie chart.
   3. The pie chart can become too cluttered and condensed if there are too many categories on it, making it unclear.
   4. (Individual answer)

B. (Suggested title) Maggie's Monthly Budget
(Individual introductory sentence)

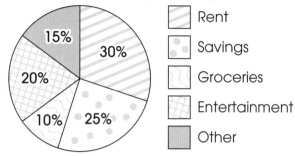

Rent 30%

Savings 15%

Groceries 20%

Entertainment 10%

Other 25%

C. (Individual writing and calculations)
D. (Individual writing, colouring, and drawing)

11   News Scripts

A. (Suggested answers)
1. Living with Robots
2. Good evening, Toronto. My name is Tom Murray and welcome to Smart News.
3. Over to you, Anne. ; Thank you, Tom. ; Back to you, Tom. ; Thank you, Anne...
4. A: Introduction: Tonight's story, "Living with Robots", is an in-depth look at life with robots by journalist Anne Harvey.
   B: Who: people living with robots
   What: an in-depth look at living with robots
   Where: Japan
   When: the present
   Why: to determine whether living with robots is a good or bad thing
   How: assess different viewpoints on the subject to allow listeners to come to a conclusion about the topic
   C: So, is living with robots a good thing or bad thing? We will let you decide.
5. Signing off, this is Tom Murray with Smart News. Good night.
B. (Individual writing)
C. (Individual writing and drawing)

Review 4

A. 1. form and content   2. pre-writing
   3. free flow of ideas   4. topical order

5. events in the order they occur in the passage of time
6. third person omniscient
7. word choice   8. tone
9. to explain   10. epistrophe
11. add, remove, move, and substitute
12. fact-check
13. checking for punctuation errors
14. an imagined future
15. mythological creatures
16. critical ; descriptive
17. evaluation of the film's strengths and weaknesses
18. statistical graph   19. a scale
20. a slogan
B. 1. Type of Word Choice: descriptive
   (Suggested examples)
   Verb: twisted ; settled
   Adjective: thoughtful ; splendid
   Adverb: dejectedly ; silently
   Tone: moving and hopeful
   (Suggested words) best ; friends ; important ; thoughtful ; beginning ; new ; adventure ; not alone ; graduation ; party ; splendid ; look forward to ; excited ; share ; unforgettable
2. A: Rhetorical Question
   B: Alliteration
   C: Simile
   (Suggested examples)
   D: Life is a novel and the end of one chapter is also the beginning of another.
   E: "It's just...we're graduating soon, and then we'll be attending humongous high schools with millions of students and we'll have metric tons of homework every day."
   F: Anne and Cleo had the rest of the year to look forward to, their graduation party to look forward to, and the splendid stretch of the summer sun to look forward to.
C. A ; B ; C ; E ; F ; G ; I ; J ; K
   (Individual writing and drawing)
D. (Individual writing)

Creative Corner – My Time Travels

Imagine you have found a time machine that allows you to travel through time and space.
Have fun exploring time and space through different text types!

Time Machine Interface

PAST

PRESENT

FUTURE

Name of Device: _____

Where I Found It: _____

_____

Places I Travelled to: _____

_____

_____

Time I Travelled to: _____

_____

_____

Write a short story about how you came across a mysterious time machine. Read the note attached to it. Describe where the machine may have come from and what led you to it.

Timescape Card

Year: _____

Place: _____

Title

_____

_____

_____

_____

_____

If you find this time machine,
On a journey you will be sent.
But as all good things must end,
It shall be passed from hand to hand.

_____

_____

_____

_____

_____

_____

_____

_____

_____

_____

_____

_____

_____

You go on a social networking site to announce your strange discovery to the science community. Create your social media profile and share a post about the machine. Remember to fill in the details for the site.

Timescape Card

Year: _____

Place: _____

www.theteleportal.pop.ca

THE TELEPORTAL

Profile   About   Sign Out

Your News Feed

My Post   Today

Like   Comment   Share

My Post   Yesterday

Like   Comment   Share

My Page

News Feed
Events
Photos
Saved Items

Chat

Advertisement

Top News

1. Alex Turner, famous watchmaker, retires at 65
2. Science Champions reach the finals
3. Sundial Mall grand opening a success

Events

Saved Items

The time machine takes you to the past. Write a play script of a scene between you and a historical figure or an ancestor of yours whom you come across. Remember to mention the year and the setting.

Timescape Card

Year: _____

Place: _____

Title

Act 1   Prologue

_____

_____

_____

_____

Act 1   Scene 1

_____

_____

_____

_____

_____

_____

_____

You expect the time machine to whisk you away to another era in the past. Instead, you find yourself at your school in the year 3050! Make a pie chart about the population dynamics of the different types of beings studying there.

Timescape Card

Year: _____

Place: _____

Title

Legend

Remember to use different colours and/or patterns for the categories. Do not put too many categories. Keep it simple!

The time machine has not yet taken you away from this futuristic version of your school. You decide to run for president of your favourite club. Design your campaign flyer.

Suggested School Clubs:

Aviation Club	Robot Rights Club	Underwater Sports Club

Timescape Card

Year: _____

Place: _____

Next, the time machine takes you to your city in the year 5000! But that is not all – the technologically advanced version of your city is built in the air! Write a science fiction story about Air City, focusing on a conflict and its resolution.

Timescape Card

Year: _____

Place: _____

Title

_____

_____

_____

_____

_____

_____

_____

_____

_____

_____

_____

_____

_____

_____

_____

_____

_____

_____

During your stay in Air City, you conduct a survey to get to know its inhabitants. Select one of the following topics and create a survey.

My Topics

◯ Transportation Preferences of the Residents of Air City

◯ Dietary Habits of the Residents of Air City

Timescape Card

Year: _____

Place: _____

Survey	Question	Always •••••	Sometimes ••◦◦◦	Never ◦◦◦◦◦	Total
1.					
2.					
3.					
4.					
5.					
6.					
7.					
8.					
9.					
10.					
11.					
12.					